DK TRAVEL GUIDES

GERMAN
PHRASE BOOK

A Dorling Kindersley Book

Dorling **DK** Kindersley

LONDON, NEW YORK, MUNICH,
MELBOURNE, AND DELHI

www.dk.com

Compiled by Lexus Ltd with Chris Stephenson and Horst Kopleck

Published in the United States by Dorling Kindersley Publishing, Inc.
95 Madison Avenue, New York, New York 10016

First American Edition 1998
Reprints with corrections 2000
4 6 8 10 9 7 5

Copyright © 1998 Dorling Kindersley Limited, London
A Penguin Company

All rights reserved under International and Pan-American
Copyright Conventions. No part of this publication may be reproduced,
stored in a retrieval system, or transmitted in any form or by any means,
electronic, mechanical, photocopying, recording, or otherwise,
without the prior written permission of the copyright owner.
Published in Great Britain by Dorling Kindersley Limited.

Dorling Kindersley books can be purchased in bulk quantities at
discounted prices for use in promotions or as premiums. We are also able to offer
special editions and personalized jackets, corporate imprints, and excerpts from all
of our books, tailored specifically to meet your own needs. To find out more,
please contact: Special Markets Department, Dorling Kindersley, Inc.,
95 Madison Avenue, New York, NY 10016; Fax: 800-600-9098.

Library of Congress Cataloging-in-Publication Data
German phrase book. -- 1st American ed.
    p.   cm. -- (Dorling Kindersley travel guides)
    Includes index.
    ISBN 0–7894–3235–8 (alk. paper)
    1. German language--Conversation and phrase books--
    English.   I. Series.
PF3121.G49   1998
383.3'421--dc21
                                                            97–47229
                                                               CIP

Picture Credits
Jacket: all special photography Clive Streeter except BRITSTOCK IFA:
Amadeus front center left above; Bernd Ducke spine top; P. Grahammer
back right; ROBERT HARDING PICTURE LIBRARY: Schuster/Jogschies front
center right bottom; ZEFA: Kotoh back left.

Printed and bound in Italy by Printer Trento Srl.

CONTENTS

PREFACE

This *Dorling Kindersley Travel Guides Phrase Book* has been compiled by experts to meet the general needs of tourists and business travelers. Arranged under headings such as Hotels, Driving, and so forth, the ample selection of useful words and phrases is supported by a 2,000-line mini-dictionary. There is also an extensive menu guide listing approximately 600 dishes or methods of cooking and presentation.

Typical replies to questions you may ask during your trip, and the signs or instructions you may see or hear, are shown in tinted boxes. In the main text, the pronunciation of German words and phrases is imitated in English sound syllables. The Introduction provides guidelines to German pronunciation.

Dorling Kindersley Travel Guides are recognized as the world's best travel guides. Each title features specially commissioned color photographs, cutaways of major buildings, 3-D aerial views and detailed maps, plus information on sights, events, hotels, restaurants, shopping, and entertainment.

Dorling Kindersley Travel Guides titles include:

Berlin · Amsterdam · Australia · Sydney · Budapest · California
Florida · Hawaii · New York · San Francisco & Northern California
Canada · France · Loire Valley · Paris · Provence · Great Britain
London · Ireland · Dublin · Scotland · Greece: Athens & the Mainland
The Greek Islands · Istanbul · Italy · Florence & Tuscany
Milan & the Lakes · Naples · Rome · Sardinia · Sicily
Venice & the Veneto · Jerusalem & the Holy Land · Mexico · Moscow
St. Petersburg · Portugal · Lisbon · Prague · South Africa
Spain · Barcelona · Madrid · Seville & Andalusia · Thailand
Vienna · Warsaw

NTRODUCTION

RONUNCIATION

√hen reading the imitated pronunciation, stress the part that
s underlined. Pronounce each syllable as if it formed part of
n English word, and you will be understood sufficiently well.
.emember the points below, and your pronunciation will be
ven closer to the correct German.

is pronounced hard as in "get."

H represents the guttural German "ch" and should sound
like the Scottish "loch" (which <u>isn't</u> "lock").

o represents the long German "u"; make this an English
"oo" as in "food" (*not* short as in "foot").

o represents the shorter German "u," as in English "took,"
"book."

) is how we imitate the German "ü," which sounds like the
"ee" in "seen" if you pronounce it with rounded lips (or
like the French "u").

w should sound like the "ow" in "cow" (*not* as in "low").

YOU" AND "I"

n most cases we have given the polite form for "you"—which
s **Sie** (*zee*). The familiar form **du** (*doo*) can also be used, but
ormally only if you are talking to someone you know well
nd would regard as a personal friend.
Questions involving "I" have sometimes been translated with
1an, for example "Can I ...?" **Kann man ...?**. Literally **man**
1eans "one" but is not a formal word as it is in English.

USEFUL EVERYDAY PHRASES

YES, NO, OK, ETC.

Yes/No
Ja/Nein
ya/nine

Good/Excellent!
Gut/Ausgezeichnet!
goot/owss-geh-tsysh-net

Don't!
Nicht!
nikht

OK
Okay
okay

That's fine
In Ordnung
in ortnoong

That's right
Stimmt
shtimmt

GREETINGS, INTRODUCTIONS

How do you do, pleased to meet you
Guten Tag, freut mich
gooten tahk froyt mikh

Good morning/good afternoon/good evening
Guten Morgen/Guten Tag/Guten Abend
gooten morgen/gooten tahk/gooten ahbent

Good night *(going to bed)*
Gute Nacht
gootuh naKHt

(leaving late at night)
Auf Wiedersehen
owf veeder-zayn

Goodbye
Auf Wiedersehen
owf veeder-zayn

How are you?
Wie geht es Ihnen?
vee gayt ess eenen

(familiar form)
Wie geht es dir?
vee gayt ess deer

My name's …
Ich heiße …
ish hice-uh

What's your name?
Wie heißen Sie?
vee hice-en zee

(familiar form)
Wie heißt du?
vee hice-t doo

What's his/her name?
Wie heißt er/sie?
vee hice-t air/zee

May I introduce …?
Darf ich Ihnen … vorstellen?
darf ish eenen … for-shtellen

This is …
Das ist …
dass ist

Hello/Hi
Hallo
hallo

Bye!
Tschüs!
chOOss

See you later
Bis später
biss shpayter

It's been nice meeting you
Es war nett, Sie kennenzulernen
ess var nett zee kennen-tsoo-lairnen

PLEASE, THANK YOU, APOLOGIES

Thank you
Danke
dankuh

No, thank you
Nein, danke
nine dankuh

Please
Bitte
bittuh

Excuse me!
Entschuldigung!
ent-shooldigoong

Sorry!
Entschuldigung!
ent-shooldigoong

I'm really sorry
Tut mir wirklich leid
toot meer veerklish lite

It was my fault/it wasn't my fault
Es war meine Schuld/Es war nicht meine Schuld
ess var mine-uh shoolt/ess var nisht mine-uh shoolt

WHERE, HOW, ASKING

Excuse me, please
Entschuldigen Sie bitte
ent-shooldigen zee bittuh

Can you tell me ...?
Können Sie mir sagen ...?
kurnen zee meer zahgen

Can I have ...?
Kann ich ... haben?
kan ish ... hahben

Would you like a ...?
Möchten Sie einen/eine/ein ...?
murshten zee ine-en/ine-uh/ine

Would you like to ...?
Möchten Sie ...?
murshten zee

Is there ... here?
Gibt es hier ...?
geept ess heer

What's that?
Was ist das?
vass ist dass

Where can I get ...?
Wo bekomme ich ...?
vo bukommuh ish

How much is it?
Was kostet das?
vass kostet dass

Where is the ...?
Wo ist der/die/das ...?
vo ist dair/dee/dass

ABOUT ONESELF

I'm from …
Ich bin aus …
ish bin owss

I'm … years old
Ich bin … Jahre alt
ish bin … yaruh allt

I'm a …
Ich bin …
ish bin

I'm married/single/divorced
Ich bin verheiratet/single/geschieden
ish bin fairhyrahtet/single/gusheeden

I have … sisters/brothers/children
Ich habe … Schwestern/Brüder/Kinder
ish hahbuh … shvestern/brooder/kinder

LIKES, DISLIKES, SOCIALIZING

I like …
Ich möchte … gern
ish murshtuh … gairn

I love …
Ich liebe …
ish leebuh …

I like swimming/traveling
Ich schwimme/reise gern
ish shvimmuh/ryzuh gairn

I don't like …
Ich möchte … nicht gern
ish murshtuh … nisht gairn

I don't like swimming/traveling
Ich schwimme/reise nicht gern
ish shvimmuh/ryzuh nisht gairn

I hate …
Ich hasse …
ish hassuh

Do you like …?
Möchten Sie …?
murshten zee

It's delicious/awful!
Es ist köstlich/furchtbar!
ess ist kurstlish/foorshtbar

I don't drink/smoke
Ich trinke/rauche nicht
ish trinkuh/rowкнuh nisht

Do you mind if I smoke?
Haben Sie etwas dagegen, wenn ich rauche?
hahben zee etvass dagaygen ven ish rowкнuh

I don't eat meat or fish
Ich esse kein Fleisch und keinen Fisch
ish essuh kine flysh oont kine-en fish

What would you like (to drink)?
Was möchten Sie (trinken)?
vass murshten zee (trinken)

I would like a …
Ich möchte gern einen/eine/ein …
ish murshtuh gairn ine-en/ine-uh/ine

Nothing for me, thanks
Nichts für mich, danke
nishts foor mish dankuh

I'll get this one
Das geht auf meine Rechnung
dass gayt owf m<u>i</u>ne-uh r<u>e</u>shnoong

Cheers!
Prost!
prohst

I would like to …
Ich möchte gern …
ish m<u>u</u>rshtuh gairn

Let's go to Stuttgart/go to the movies
Sollen wir nach Stuttgart fahren/ins Kino gehen?
z<u>o</u>llen veer nahкн sht<u>oo</u>tgart f<u>a</u>ren/inss k<u>ee</u>no g<u>a</u>y-en

Let's go swimming/for a walk
Sollen wir schwimmen/spazieren gehen?
z<u>o</u>llen veer shv<u>i</u>mmen/shpats<u>ee</u>ren g<u>a</u>y-en

What's the weather like?
Wie ist das Wetter?
vee ist dass v<u>e</u>tter

The weather's awful
Das Wetter ist furchtbar
dass v<u>e</u>tter ist f<u>oo</u>rshtbar

It's pouring down
Es gießt
ess geest

It's really hot/sunny
Es ist wirklich heiß/sonnig
ess ist v<u>ee</u>rklish hice/z<u>o</u>nnish

HELP, PROBLEMS *(see also* EMERGENCIES *p108)*

Can you help me?
Können Sie mir helfen?
k<u>u</u>rnen zee meer h<u>e</u>lfen

I don't understand
Ich verstehe nicht
ish fairsht<u>a</u>yuh nisht

Do you speak English/French?
Sprechen Sie Englisch/Französisch?
shpr<u>e</u>shen zee <u>e</u>ng-lish/frants<u>ur</u>-zish

Does anyone here speak English?
Spricht hier jemand Englisch?
shprisht heer y<u>a</u>ymant <u>e</u>ng-lish

I can't speak German
Ich spreche kein Deutsch
ish shpr<u>e</u>shuh kine doytsh

I don't know
Ich weiß nicht
ish vice nisht

What's wrong?
Stimmt etwas nicht?
shtimmt <u>e</u>tvass nisht

Please speak more slowly
Sprechen Sie bitte etwas langsamer
shpr<u>e</u>shen zee b<u>i</u>ttuh <u>e</u>tvass l<u>a</u>ngzahmer

Please write it down for me
Könnten Sie es mir bitte aufschreiben?
k<u>u</u>rnten zee ess meer b<u>i</u>ttuh <u>ow</u>f-shryben

I'm lost
Ich habe mich verlaufen
ish h<u>a</u>hbuh mish fairl<u>ow</u>fen

(driving)
Ich habe mich verfahren
ish h<u>a</u>hbuh mish fairf<u>a</u>ren

Where is the US/British embassy?
Wo finde ich die Amerikanische/Britische Botschaft?
voh f<u>i</u>nduh ish dee amerikanish<u>uh</u>/british<u>uh</u> b<u>o</u>htshaft?

TALKING TO RECEPTIONISTS, ETC.

I have an appointment with …
Ich habe eine Verabredung mit …
ish hahbuh ine-uh fairap-raydoong mit

I'd like to see …
Ich möchte gern … sprechen
ish murshtuh gairn … shpreshen

Here's my card
Hier ist meine Karte
heer ist mine-uh kartuh

My company is …
Meine Firma ist …
mine-uh feerma ist

May I use the phone/photocopier/fax machine?
Kann ich das Telefon/das Fotokopiergerät/das Faxgerät benutzen?
kan ish dass telefohn/dass fotokopeargerayt/dass faxgerayt bunootsen

Is there wheelchair access?
Kann man dort mit einem Rollstuhl hinein?
kan man dohrt mit ine-nem rollshtuhl hin-ine?

Are guide dogs allowed?
Sind Blindenhunde erlaubt?
zint blindenhoonduh airlowpt?

THINGS YOU'LL HEAR

Achtung!	attention, look out!
auf Wiedersehen	goodbye
bedienen Sie sich	help yourself
bis später	see you later
bitte	please
bitte?	excuse me?

→

bitte (schön/sehr)	here you are, you're welcome
bitte (schön/sehr)?	what will it be?
	is it?
	can I help you?
danke	thanks
danke gleichfalls	the same to you
Entschuldigung	excuse me
genau	exactly
gut	good
guten Tag, freut mich	how do you do, nice to meet you
gute Reise	have a good trip
ich verstehe nicht	I don't understand
ich weiß nicht	I don't know
schöne Grüße an ...	give my regards to ...
stimmt	that's right
tschüs	bye
tut mir wirklich leid!	I'm so sorry!
Verzeihung	excuse me
vielen Dank	thank you very much
wie bitte?	what did you say?
wie geht es Ihnen?	how are you?
wie geht's?	how are things?
wirklich?	is that so?
	really?

THINGS YOU'LL SEE

Abfall	litter
auf Wiedersehen	goodbye
Aufzug	elevator
außer	except
außer Betrieb	out of order
Ausgang	exit

15

USEFUL EVERYDAY PHRASES

Auskunft	information
belegt	no vacancies
besetzt	occupied
Besuchszeiten	visiting hours
bitte nicht …	please do not …
Damen	women
drücken	push
Eingang	entrance
Eintritt	entry
Eintritt frei	free admission
Erdgeschoß	ground floor
Feiertag	national holiday
frisch gestrichen	wet paint
Fußgänger	pedestrians
Gefahr	danger
geöffnet	open
geschlossen	closed
Herren	men
kein(e) …	no …; none
kein Zutritt	no admittance
nicht …	do not …
Nichtraucher	no smoking
Notausgang	emergency exit
nur …	only …
Öffnungszeiten	opening times
Raucher	smokers
Straße	street
Stock	floor, story
Tiefgeschoß	basement
untersagt	prohibited
verboten	forbidden
Vorsicht	take care
ziehen	pull
Zoll	customs
zu verkaufen	for sale
zu vermieten	for rent

COLLOQUIALISMS

You may hear these: to use some of them yourself could be risky!

Alles klar!	fine, great
Arschloch	S.O.B.
bekloppt	crazy
bescheuert	crazy
besoffen	drunk, smashed
Blödsinn	nonsense
doof	stupid
du lieber Gott!	good God!
du spinnst wohl!	you've got to be joking!
	you're out of your mind!
Kumpel	pal
Mann!	boy!
Mensch!	wow!
nee	nope
Ossi	East German
sauer	pissed off
Schnauze!	shut your mouth!
Schwachkopf	idiot
Schwachsinn	trash
Sonntagsfahrer!	Sunday driver!
Spitze	fantastic
stark	great
super	great
toll!	tremendous!
Typ	guy
Unverschämtheit	bold, nerve
verdammt noch mal!	oh, hell!
Wahnsinn!	fantastic!
Wessi	West German

DAYS, MONTHS, SEASONS

Sunday	Sonntag	_zontahk_
Monday	Montag	_mohntahk_
Tuesday	Dienstag	_deenstahk_
Wednesday	Mittwoch	_mitvoкн_
Thursday	Donnerstag	_donnerstahk_
Friday	Freitag	_frytahk_
Saturday	Samstag,	_zamstahk,_
	Sonnabend	_zonnahbent_
January	Januar	_yanooar_
February	Februar	_faybrooar_
March	März	_mairts_
April	April	_april_
May	Mai	_my_
June	Juni	_yoonee_
July	Juli	_yoolee_
August	August	_owgoost_
September	September	_zeptember_
October	Oktober	_oktober_
November	November	_november_
December	Dezember	_daytsember_
Spring	Frühling	_frooling_
Summer	Sommer	_zommer_
Fall	Herbst	_hairpst_
Winter	Winter	_vinter_
Christmas	Weihnachten	_vynaкнten_
Christmas Eve	Heiligabend	_hylish-ahbent_
New Year	Neujahr	_noy-yar_
New Year's Eve	Silvester	_zilvester_
Easter	Ostern	_ohstern_
Good Friday	Karfreitag	_karfrytahk_
Pentecost	Pfingsten	_pfingsten_

NUMBERS

0	null *nool*	10	zehn *tsayn*
1	eins *ine-ss*	11	elf *elf*
2	zwei *tsvy*	12	zwölf *tsvurlf*
3	drei *dry*	13	dreizehn *dry-tsayn*
4	vier *feer*	14	vierzehn *veer-tsayn*
5	fünf *fOOnf*	15	fünfzehn *fOOnf-tsayn*
6	sechs *zex*	16	sechzehn *zesh-tsayn*
7	sieben *zeeben*	17	siebzehn *zeep-tsayn*
8	acht *aKHt*	18	achtzehn *aKHt-tsayn*
9	neun *noyn*	19	neunzehn *noyn-tsayn*

20	zwanzig *tsvantsish*
21	einundzwanzig *ine-oont-tsvantsish*
22	zweiundzwanzig *tsvy-oont-tsvantsish*
30	dreißig *drysish*
40	vierzig *feertsish*
50	fünfzig *fOOnftsish*
60	sechzig *zeshtsish*
70	siebzig *zeeptsish*
80	achtzig *aKHtsish*
90	neunzig *noyntsish*
100	hundert *hoondert*
110	hundertzehn *hoondert-tsayn*
200	zweihundert *tsvy-hoondert*
1,000	tausend *towzent*
10,000	zehntausend *tsayn-towzent*
100,000	hunderttausend *hoondert-towzent*
1,000,000	eine Million *ine-uh mill-yohn*

Ordinal numbers are formed by adding **-te**, or **-ste** if the number ends in **-ig**. For example, **fünfte** (*fOOnftuh*, "fifth"), **zwanzigste** (*tsvantsishstuh*, "twentieth"). Exceptions are: **erste** (*airstuh*, "first"), **dritte** (*drittuh*, "third"), and **siebte** (*zeeptuh*, "seventh").

TIME

TELLING TIME

To say the hour in German use the word **Uhr** (*oor*) preceded by the appropriate number; for example: **neun Uhr** (*noyn oor*) is "nine o'clock." The 24-hour clock is used much more commonly in Germany.

The word for "past" is **nach** (*nahkh*). So **zehn nach neun** (*tsayn nahkh noyn*) is "ten past nine." The word for "to" is **vor** (*for*). So **zehn vor neun** (*tsayn for noyn*) is "ten to nine." The word for "(a) quarter" is **viertel** (*feertel*). So **viertel nach/vor neun** (*feertel nahkh/for noyn*) is "(a) quarter past/to nine."

The important thing to remember when telling time is that, when talking about the half hour, Germans count back from the next full hour, so that, for example, "9:30" is said in German as "half ten." So **es ist halb zehn** (*ess ist halp tsayn*) means "it's 9:30." Think "half to" instead of thirty minutes past the hour.

USEFUL WORDS AND PHRASES

today	heute	*hoytuh*
yesterday	gestern	*gestern*
tomorrow	morgen	*morgen*
the day before yesterday	vorgestern	*forgestern*
the day after tomorrow	übermorgen	*übermorgen*
this week	diese Woche	*deezuh vokhuh*
last week	letzte Woche	*letstuh vokhuh*
next week	nächste Woche	*naykstuh vokhuh*
this morning	heute morgen	*hoytuh morgen*
this afternoon	heute nachmittag	*hoytuh nahkhmit-tahk*
this evening	heute abend	*hoytuh ahbent*
tonight	heute abend	*hoytuh ahbent*

yesterday afternoon	gestern nachmittag	*gestern nahкнmit-tahk*
last night		
(*last evening*)	gestern Abend	*gestern ahbent*
(*late at night*)	gestern Nacht	*gestern naкнt*
tomorrow morning	morgen früh	*morgen frœ*
tomorrow night	morgen abend	*morgen ahbent*
in three days	in drei Tagen	*in dry tahgen*
three days ago	vor drei Tagen	*for dry tahgen*
late	spät	*shpayt*
early	früh	*frœ*
soon	bald	*balt*
later on	später	*shpayter*
at the moment	im Moment	*im moment*
second	die Sekunde	*zekoonduh*
minute	die Minute	*minootuh*
one minute	eine Minute	*ine-uh minootuh*
two minutes	zwei Minuten	*tsvy minooten*
quarter of an hour	eine Viertelstunde	*feertelshtoonduh*
half an hour	eine halbe Stunde	*halbuh shtoonduh*
three quarters of an hour	eine Dreiviertel-stunde	*dryfeertel-shtoonduh*
hour	die Stunde	*shtoonduh*
day	der Tag	*tahk*
everyday	jeden Tag	*yayden tahk*
all day	den ganzen Tag	*dayn gantsen tahk*
the next day	am nächsten Tag	*am nayksten tahk*
week	die Woche	*voкнuh*
two weeks	zwei Wochen	*tsvy voкнen*
month	der Monat	*mohnaht*
year	das Jahr	*yar*
what time is it?	wie spät ist es?	*vee shpayt ist ess*
am	morgens	*morgens*

pm	nachmittags	*nahкнmittahks*
(in the evening)	abends	*ahbents*
one o'clock	ein Uhr	*ine oor*
ten past one	zehn nach eins	*tsayn nahкн ine-ss*
quarter past one	viertel nach eins	*feertel nahкн ine-ss*
1:30	halb zwei	*halp tsvy*
twenty to two	zwanzig vor zwei	*tsvantsish for tsvy*
quarter to two	viertel vor zwei	*feertel for tsvy*
13:00	dreizehn Uhr	*dry-tsayn oor*
16:30	sechzehn Uhr	*zesh-tsayn oor*
	dreißig	*drysish*
at 5:30	um halb sechs	*oom halp zex*

HOTELS

Hotels in Germany are categorized by the international star-rating system, with the range of services and level of luxury corresponding to what you would expect to find at home. If you're looking for more basic accommodations, you could try a **Gasthof**, **Gasthaus**, or **Pension**. A **Gasthof** or **Gasthaus** will often be an establishment with a restaurant on the ground floor and rooms on the other floors—a traditional inn. The signs "**Zimmer frei**" or "**Fremdenzimmer**" mean that rooms are available and, if on display in the window of a private house, will indicate a bed and breakfast type of accommodation.

USEFUL WORDS AND PHRASES

balcony	der Balkon	*balkong*
bath *(tub)*	die Badewanne	*bahduh-vannuh*
bathroom	das Bad	*baht*
bed	das Bett	*bet*
bed and breakfast	Übernachtung mit Frühstück	*ωbernaκнtoong mit frωshtωk*
bedroom	das (Schlaf)zimmer	*(shlahf)tsimmer*
bill	die Rechnung	*reshnoong*
breakfast	das Frühstück	*frωshtωk*
dining room	der Speisesaal	*shpyzuh-zahl*
dinner *(evening)*	das Abendessen	*ahbentessen*
double bed	das Doppelbett	*doppelbet*
double room	das Doppelzimmer	*doppeltsimmer*
elevator	der Aufzug, der Lift	*owf-tsook, lift*
foyer	das Foyer	*fwa-yay*
full board	Vollpension	*follpangz-yohn*
guesthouse	die Pension	*pangz-yohn*
half board	Halbpension	*halp-pangz-yohn*
hotel	das Hotel	*hotel*
key	der Schlüssel	*shlωssel*
lounge	der Aufenthaltsraum	*owfenthaltsrowm*

lunch	das Mittagessen	*mittahkessen*
maid	das Zimmermädchen	*tsimmer-maydshen*
manager	der Geschäftsführer	*gushefts-fOOrer*
parking lot	der Parkplatz	*parkplats*
receipt	die Quittung	*kvittoong*
reception	der Empfang	*empfang*
receptionist	der Empfangschef	*empfangs-shef*
(woman)	die Empfangsdame	*empfangs-dahmuh*
room	das Zimmer	*tsimmer*
room service	der Zimmerservice	*tsimmer-"service"*
shower	die Dusche	*dooshuh*
single bed	das Einzelbett	*ine-tselbet*
single room	das Einzelzimmer	*ine-tsel-tsimmer*
sink	das Waschbecken	*vashbecken*
toilet	die Toilette	*twalettuh*
twin room	das Zweibettzimmer	*tsvybet-tsimmer*

Do you have any vacancies?
Haben Sie Zimmer frei?
hahben zee tsimmer fry

I have a reservation
Ich habe ein Zimmer reserviert
ish hahbuh ine tsimmer rezerveert

I'd like a single room
Ich möchte ein Einzelzimmer
ish murshtuh ine ine-tsel-tsimmer

I'd like a room with a bathroom/balcony
Ich möchte ein Zimmer mit Bad/Balkon
ish murshtuh ine tsimmer mit baht/balkong

Is there satellite/cable TV in the rooms?
Gibt es Satelliten/Kabel fernsehen in den Zimmern?
gipt as zateleeten/kahbel fairnzayhen in den tsimmern?

I'd like a room for one night/three nights
Ich möchte ein Zimmer für eine Nacht/drei Nächte
ish murshtuh ine tsimmer foor ine-uh naкнt/dry neshtuh

What is the charge per night?
Was kostet es pro Nacht?
vass kostet ess pro naкнt

I don't know yet how long I'll stay
Ich weiß noch nicht, wie lange ich bleiben werde
ish vice noкн nisht vee lang-uh ish blyben vairduh

When is breakfast/dinner?
Wann wird das Frühstück/Abendessen serviert?
vann veert dass frooshtook/ahbentessen zairveert

Please wake/call me at … o'clock
Bitte wecken Sie mich um … Uhr
bittuh vecken zee mish oom … oor

Can I have breakfast in my room?
Können Sie mir das Frühstück auf mein Zimmer bringen?
kurnen zee meer dass frooshtook owf mine tsimmer bring-en

I'll be back at … o'clock
Ich bin um … Uhr wieder da
ish bin oom … oor veeder da

My room number is …
Meine Zimmernummer ist …
mine-uh tsimmer-noommer ist …

I'd like to have some laundry done
Ich möchte gern meine Wäsche waschen lassen
ish murshtuh gairn mine-uh veshuh vashen lassen

My reservation was for a double room
Ich hatte ein Doppelzimmer reserviert
ish hattuh ine doppeltsimmer rezerveert

I asked for a room with a private bathroom
Ich hatte um ein Zimmer mit eigenem Bad gebeten
ish hattuh oom ine tsimmer mit ige-enem baht gubayten

I need a light bulb
Ich brauche eine Glühbirne
ish browкнuh ine-uh glⱺbeernuh

The lamp is broken
Die Lampe ist kaputt
dee lampuh ist kapoot

There is no toilet paper in the bathroom
Im Badezimmer ist kein Toilettenpapier
im bahduh-tsimmer ist kine twaletten-papeer

The window won't open
Das Fenster geht nicht auf
dass fenster gayt nisht owf

There isn't any hot water
Es gibt kein warmes Wasser
ess geept kine varmess vasser

The outlet in the bathroom doesn't work
Die Steckdose im Badezimmer funktioniert nicht
dee shtek-dohzuh im bahduh-tsimmer foonkts-yoneert nisht

I'm leaving tomorrow
Ich reise morgen ab
ish ryzuh morgen ap

When do I have to vacate the room?
Bis wann muß ich das Zimmer räumen?
biss van mooss ish dass tsimmer roymen

Can I have the bill, please?
Kann ich bitte die Rechnung haben?
kan ish bittuh dee reshnoong hahben

I'll pay by credit card
Ich zahle mit Kreditkarte
ish tsahluh mit kredeetkartuh

I'll pay cash
Ich zahle in bar
ish tsahluh in bar

Can you get me a taxi?
Können Sie mir ein Taxi bestellen?
kurnen zee meer ine taxi bushtellen

Can you recommend another hotel?
Können Sie ein anderes Hotel empfehlen?
kurnen zee ine anderess hotel empfaylen

THINGS YOU'LL SEE

Aufzug	elevator
Bad	bath
belegt	no vacancies
Doppelzimmer	double room
drücken	push
Dusche	shower
Eingang	entrance
Einzelzimmer	single room
Empfang	reception, lobby
Erdgeschoß	first floor
erster Stock	second floor
Fahrstuhl	elevator
Fremdenzimmer	room(s) to rent
Frühstück	breakfast
Gasthaus, Gasthof	inn
Halbpension	half board
kein Zutritt	no admission
Mittagessen	lunch
Notausgang	emergency exit

→

nur für Gäste	patrons only
Parkplatz	parking lot
Pension	guesthouse
Rechnung	bill
Speisesaal	restaurant, dining room
Treppe	stairs
Übernachtung	night
Übernachtung mit Frühstück	bed and breakfast
voll belegt	no vacancies
Vollpension	full board
ziehen	pull
Zimmer frei	vacancy
Zuschlag	supplement
Zweibettzimmer	twin room
zweiter Stock	third floor

THINGS YOU'LL HEAR

Mit oder ohne Bad?
With or without a bath?

Tut mir leid, wir sind voll belegt
I'm sorry, we're full

Es sind keine Einzelzimmer/Doppelzimmer mehr frei
There are no single/double rooms left

Für wie lange?
For how long?

Wie möchten Sie zahlen?
How would you like to pay?

Könnten Sie bitte im voraus bezahlen
Could you please pay in advance

Sie müssen das Zimmer bis zwölf Uhr räumen
You must vacate the room by noon

CAMPING AND TRAILER TRAVEL

Germany has over 2,500 well-equipped campsites, most
of which are open from May through September. In some
winter sports areas you will find sites open all year round.

There are also more than 600 youth hostels throughout the
country, and mountain shelters or **Berghütten** (*bairk-hꝏtten*)
provided by hiking clubs, which also mark the more interesting
trail routes.

Useful Words and Phrases

backpack	der Rucksack	*rookzak*
bucket	der Eimer	*ime-er*
camper (RV)	der Wohnwagen	*vohn-vahgen*
camper site	der Campingplatz	*kemping-plats*
campfire	das Lagerfeuer	*lahger-foy-er*
campsite	der Campingplatz	*kemping-plats*
go camping	zelten gehen	*tselten gay-en*
cooking utensils	die Kochgeräte	*koкн-guraytuh*
drinking water	das Trinkwasser	*trinkvasser*
groundcloth	die Zeltbodenplane	*tseltbohden-plahnuh*
hitchhike	trampen	*trempen*
rope	das Seil	*zile*
saucepans	die Kochtöpfe	*koкн-turpfuh*
sleeping bag	der Schlafsack	*shlahfzak*
tent	das Zelt	*tselt*
trash	der Abfall	*apfal*
youth hostel	die Jugendherberge	*yoogent-hairbairguh*

Can I camp here?
Kann man hier zelten?
kan man heer tselten

Can we park the camper (RV) here?
Können wir den Wohnwagen hier abstellen?
kurnen veer dayn vohn-vahgen heer apshtellen

Where is the nearest campsite/camper site?
Wo ist der nächste Campingplatz?
vo ist dair naykstuh kemping-plats

What is the charge per night?
Was kostet es pro Nacht?
vass kostet ess pro nakht

How much is it for a week?
Was ist der Preis für eine Woche?
vass ist dair price foor ine-uh vokhuh

I want to stay for only one night
Ich möchte nur eine Nacht bleiben
ish murshtuh noor ine-uh nakht blyben

We're leaving tomorrow
Wir fahren morgen ab
veer faren morgen ap

Where is the kitchen?
Wo ist die Küche?
vo ist dee kooshuh

Can I light a fire here?
Kann man hier ein Feuer machen?
kan man heer ine foy-er makhen

Where can I get …?
Wo bekomme ich …?
vo bukommuh ish

Is there drinking water here?
Gibt es hier Trinkwasser?
geept ess heer trinkvasser

THINGS YOU'LL SEE

Anhänger	trailer
Ausweis	pass, identity card
Benutzung	use
Bettdecken	bedding
Campingplatz	campsite
Dusche	shower
Feuer	fire
Gebühren	charges
Jugendherberge	youth hostel
Küche	kitchen
Licht	light
Schlafraum	dormitory
Schlafsäcke	sleeping bags
Trinkwasser	drinking water
Wohnwagen	camper (RV)
Zelt	tent
Zelten verboten	no camping
Zeltplatz	campsite
zu verleihen	to borrow
zu vermieten	to rent

VILLAS AND APARTMENTS

You may be asked to pay for certain "extras" not included in the original price. You might want to ask if electricity, gas, etc., is included. It's a good idea to ask about an inventory of household goods at the start, rather than be told later something is missing just as you are about to leave. You may be asked for a deposit—make sure you get a receipt for this.

USEFUL WORDS AND PHRASES

agent	der Vertreter	*fairtrayter*
bathtub	das Bad	*baht*
bathroom	das Badezimmer	*bahduhtsimmer*
bedroom	das Zimmer	*tsimmer*
blind	das Rollo	*rollo*
blocked	verstopft	*fairshtopft*
boiler	der Boiler	*boiler*
break (*something*)	zerbrechen	*tsairbreshen*
broken	kaputt	*kapoot*
caretaker	der Hausmeister	*howss-myster*
central heating	die Zentralheizung	*tsentrahl-hytsoong*
cleaner	die Reinemachefrau	*rynumaкниfrow*
deposit	die Anzahlung	*antsahloong*
drain	der Abfluß	*apflooss*
electrician	der Elektriker	*aylektriker*
electricity	der Strom	*shtrohm*
faucet	der Hahn	*hahn*
fusebox	der Sicherungskasten	*zisheroongskasten*
garbage can	die Mülltonne	*mooltonnuh*
gas	das Gas	*gahss*
grill	der Grill	*grill*
heater	das Heizgerät	*hytsgurayt*
iron	das Bügeleisen	*boogel-ize-en*
ironing board	das Bügelbrett	*boogelbret*

eys	die Schlüssel	*shlÿssel*
itchen	die Küche	*kÿshuh*
eak	die undichte Stelle	*oondishtuh shtelluh*
ght	das Licht	*lisht*
ght bulb	die Glühbirne	*glÿbeernuh*
ving room	das Wohnzimmer	*vohntsimmer*
naid	die Hausangestellte	*howss-angushtelltuh*
illow	das Kopfkissen	*kopfkissen*
illowcase	der Kopfkissenbezug	*kopfkissenbutsook*
lumber	der Klempner	*klempner*
eceipt	die Quittung	*kvittoong*
efrigerator	der Kühlschrank	*kÿlshrank*
efund	die Rückerstattung	*rÿkairshtattoong*
heets	die Bettlaken	*bet-lahken*
hower	die Dusche	*dooshuh*
ink	das Waschbecken	*vash-becken*
topper	der Absperrhahn	*apshpairhahn*
tove	der Herd	*hairt*
wimming pool	der Swimmingpool	*swimming pool*
oilet	die Toilette	*twalettuh*
owel	das Handtuch	*hant-tOOKH*
vashing machine	die Waschmaschine	*vash-masheenuh*
vater	das Wasser	*vasser*
vater heater	das Heißwassergerät	*hice-vassergurayt*

Does the price include gas/electricity/cleaning?
st der Preis einschließlich Gas/Strom/Reinigung?
st dair price ine-shleesslish gahss/shtrohm/rynigoong

Do I need to sign an inventory?
Muß ich eine Bestandsliste unterschreiben?
tooss ish ine-uh bushtants-listuh oontershryben

Where is this item?
Wo ist das?
o ist dass

Please take it off the inventory
Bitte streichen Sie es von der Bestandsliste
bittuh shtryshen zee ess fon dair bushtants-listuh

We've broken this
Das ist uns kaputtgegangen
dass ist oonss kapoot-gugang-en

This was broken when we arrived
Es war schon kaputt, als wir ankamen
ess var shohn kapoot alss veer ankahmen

This was missing when we arrived
Das fehlte schon, als wir ankamen
dass fayltuh shohn alss veer ankahmen

May I have my deposit back?
Kann ich meine Anzahlung zurückbekommen?
kan ish mine-uh antsahloong tsoorook-bukommen

May we have an extra bed?
Können Sie uns ein extra Bett geben?
kurnen zee oonss ine extra bett gayben

May we have more dishes/silverware?
Können wir mehr Geschirr/Besteck bekommen?
kurnen veer mair gusheer/bushtek bukommen

Where is …?
Wo ist …?
vo ist

When does the maid come?
Wann kommt die Hausangestellte?
van kommt dee howss-angushtelltuh

Where can I buy/find …?
Wo kann ich … kaufen/finden?
vo kan ish … kowfen/finden

When is the bank/supermarket open?
Wann hat die Bank/der Supermarkt auf?
an hat dee bank/dair zoopermarkt owf

How does the water heater work?
Wie funktioniert das Heißwassergerät?
ee foonkts-yoneert dass hice-vassergurayt

Do you do ironing/baby-sitting?
Haben Sie einen Bügeldienst/Babysitterdienst?
ahben zee ine-en bwgeldeenst/'babysitter'-deenst

Do you make lunch/dinner?
Können Sie für uns mittags/abends kochen?
urnen zee fwr oonss mittahks/ahbents koкнen

Do we have to pay extra, or is this included in the price?
Ist das extra oder im Preis einbegriffen?
st dass extra ohder im price ine-bugriffen

The shower doesn't work
Die Dusche funktioniert nicht
ee dooshuh foonkts-yoneert nisht

The sink is blocked
Der Abfluß ist verstopft
air apflooss ist fairshtopft

The sink/toilet is leaking
Der Abfluß/die Toilette leckt
air apflooss/dee twalettuh lekt

There's a burst pipe
Ein Rohr ist geplatzt
ne ror ist guplatst

The garbage has not been collected for a week
Der Müll ist seit einer Woche nicht abgeholt worden
air mwl ist zite ine-er voкнuh nisht apguhohlt vorden

35

There's no electricity/gas/water
Es gibt keinen Strom/kein Gas/kein Wasser
ess geept kine-en shtrohm/kine gahss/kine vasser

Our bottled gas has run out—how do we get a new canister?
Unsere Gasflasche ist leer—wo bekommen wir eine neue?
oonzeruh gahss-flashuh ist lair vo bukommen veer ine-uh noyuh

Can you fix it today?
Können Sie es heute reparieren lassen?
kurnen zee ess hoytuh repareeren lassen

What is the name and telephone number of the nearest doctor/dentist?
Was ist der Name und die Telefonnummer des nächsten Arztes/Zahnarztes?
vass ist dair nahmuh oont dee telefohn-noommer des nayksten artstess/tsahn-artstess

Send your bill to …
Schicken Sie die Rechnung an …
shicken zee dee reshnoong an

I'm staying at …
Ich wohne in …
ish vohnuh in

Thanks for looking after us so well
Vielen Dank, daß Sie sich so nett um uns gekümmert haben
feelen dank dass zee zish zo nett oom oonss gukuemmert hahben

See you again next year
Bis nächstes Jahr
biss naykstess yar

DRIVING

Drive on the right, pass on the left. On divided highways you may remain in the left-hand lane if there is dense traffic on your right, but when lines of traffic have formed in all lanes you are allowed to drive faster in a right-hand lane. If you happen to be in a left-hand lane you may move to the right only in order to turn off, stop, or follow directional arrows.

Traffic coming from the right has priority at intersections and junctions wherever there is no priority sign or traffic light, unless entering the main road from a parking lot, service station, private road, path, or forest track. Your right of way is signaled by a yellow diamond or the more familiar arrow inside a red triangle. The former gives you priority for some distance ahead while the latter applies to the next intersection only. An inverted red triangle or an octagonal "STOP" sign means that you must yield. You must stop even if there is no traffic.

In built-up areas a speed limit of 31 mph (50 km/h) is shown by the town's name on a yellow plate. The same plate with a diagonal red stripe marks the end of both limit and area. On other roads, except divided highways, there is a speed limit of 62 mph (100 km/h). Heavier vehicles—trucks, buses, cars towing trailers, or large trailers themselves—are restricted to 50 mph (80 km/h) on all roads and autobahns. There is no speed limit on the autobahns for cars (with the exception of some roads in what used to be East Germany).

It is illegal to drive with only your parking lights on. Motorcyclists must use headlights at all times.

SOME COMMON ROAD SIGNS

Achtung	watch out
Anlieger frei	residents only
Autobahn	highway
Autobahndreieck	highway intersection

→

Autobahnkreuz	highway junction
Bahnübergang	train crossing
Baustelle	roadwork
bei Frost Glatteisgefahr	icy in cold weather
bitte einordnen	get in lane
Bundesautobahn	federal highway
Bundesstraße	main road
Durchgangsverkehr	through traffic
Einbahnstraße	one-way street
eingeschränktes Halteverbot	restricted parking
Fahrradweg	cycle path
Frostschäden	frost damage
Fußgänger	pedestrians
Fußgängerzone	shopping center
Gefahr	danger
gefährliche Kreuzung	dangerous crossing
gefährliche Kurve	dangerous bend
Gegenverkehr hat Vorfahrt	oncoming traffic has right of way
gesperrt für Fahrzeuge aller Art	closed to all vehicles
Glatteis	black ice
Halteverbot	no stopping
Höchstgeschwindigkeit	maximum speed
keine Zufahrt	no entry
Kreuzung	intersection
Kriechspur	slow lane
kurvenreiche Strecke	bends
Landstraße	two-lane road, one-lane road
langsam fahren	drive slowly
Nebel	fog
nur für Busse	buses only
Parken nur mit Parkscheibe	parking permit holders only
Parkverbot	no parking

→

Radweg kreuzt	bicycle lane crossing	
Raststätte	service area	
rechts fahren	keep to the right	
Sackgasse	no through road	
schlechte Fahrbahn	bad surface	
Schule	school	
Schwerlastverkehr	heavy vehicles	
Seitenstreifen nicht befahrbar	soft shoulder	
Stadtmitte	town center	
starkes Gefälle	steep gradient	
Stau	traffic jam	
Steinschlag	falling rocks	
Straßenbahn	tram	
Überholen verboten	no passing	
Umgehungsstraße	by-pass	
Umleitung	detour	
Unebenheiten	uneven surface	
verengte Fahrbahn	road narrows	
Vorfahrt gewähren	yield	
Vorfahrtsstraße	drivers on this road have priority	
Zoll	customs	

USEFUL WORDS AND PHRASES

brake	die Bremse	*bremzuh*
breakdown	die Panne	*pannuh*
car	das Auto	*owto*
clutch	die Kupplung	*kooploong*
drive (verb)	fahren	*faren*
engine	der Motor	*mohtor*
exhaust	der Auspuff	*owss-poof*
fanbelt	der Keilriemen	*kile-reemen*
garage (repairs)	die Werkstatt	*vairkshtat*
gas	das Benzin	*bentseen*

gas station	die Tankstelle	*tankstelle*
gear	der Gang	*gang*
gears/gear shift	das Getriebe	*gutreebuh*
headlights	die Scheinwerfer	*shine-vairfer*
highway	die Autobahn	*owtoh-bahn*
hood	die Motorhaube	*mohtorhow-buh*
intersection	die Kreuzung	*kroytsoong*
(*highway entry*)	die Auffahrt	*owf-fart*
(*highway exit*)	die Ausfahrt	*owss-fart*
license	der Führerschein	*fＶrer-shine*
license plate	das Nummernschild	*noommernshilt*
mirror	der Spiegel	*shpeegel*
motorcycle	das Motorrad	*motor-raht*
parking lot	der Parkplatz	*parkplats*
(*multi-story*)	der Parkhaus	*parkhowss*
parking meter	die Parkuhr	*park-oor*
parking ticket	der Strafzettel	*shtrahf-tsettel*
road	die Straße	*shtrahssuh*
spare parts	die Ersatzteile	*airzats-tile-uh*
spark plug	die Zündkerze	*tsＶnt-kairtsuh*
speed	die Geschwindigkeit	*gushvindish-kite*
speed limit	die Geschwindigkeits-	*gushvindish-kites-*
	beschränkung	*bushrenkoong*
speedometer	der Tacho(meter)	*taкно(mayter)*
steering wheel	das Lenkrad	*lenkraht*
taillights	das Rücklicht	*rooklisht*
tire	der Reifen	*rife-en*
tow	abschleppen	*apshleppen*
traffic lights	die Ampel	*ampel*
trailer	der Anhänger,	*anheng-er,*
	der Wohnwagen	*vohn-vahgen*
truck	der Lastwagen	*last-vahgen*
trunk	der Kofferaum	*kofferrowm*
turn signal	der Blinker	*blinker*
van	der Lieferwagen	*leefer-vahgen*
wheel	das Rad	*raht*

windshield	die Windschutz-scheibe	*vint-shoots-shybuh*
windshield wiper	der Scheibenwischer	*shyben-visher*

I'd like some gas/oil/water
Ich brauche Benzin/Öl/Wasser
ish browкнuh bentseen/url/vasser

Fill it up, please!
Volltanken bitte!
folltanken bittuh

Twenty liters of super unleaded, please
Zwanzig Liter Super bleifrei bitte
tsvantsish leeter zooper bly-fry bittuh

Would you check the tires, please?
Könnten Sie bitte die Reifen überprüfen?
kurnten zee bittuh dee rife-en ωberprωfen

Do you do repairs?
Machen Sie Reparaturen?
maкнen zee reparatooren

Can you repair the clutch?
Können Sie die Kupplung reparieren?
kurnen zee dee kooploong repareeren

There is something wrong with the engine
Mit dem Motor stimmt etwas nicht
mit daym mohtor shtimmt etvass nisht

The engine is overheating
Der Motor ist heißgelaufen
dair mohtor ist hice-gulowfen

I need a new tire
Ich brauche einen neuen Reifen
ish browкнuh ine-en noyen rife-en

Can you replace this?
Haben Sie dafür einen Ersatz?
hahben zee dafœr ine-en airsats

The turn signal is not working
Der Blinker funktioniert nicht
dair blinker foonkts-yoneert nisht

How long will it take?
Wie lange wird das dauern?
vee lang-uh veert dass dowern

Where can I park?
Wo kann ich parken?
vo kan ish parken

May I park here?
Kann ich hier parken?
kan ish heer parken

I'd like to rent a car
Ich möchte ein Auto mieten
ish murshtuh ine owto meeten

I'd like an automatic/a manual
Ich möchte ein Auto mit Automatik/mit Handschaltung
ish murshtuh ine owto mit owtomahtik/mit hantshaltoong

For one day/two days/one week
Für einen Tag/zwei Tage/eine Woche
fœr ine-en tahk/tsvy tahguh/ine-uh voкнuh

How much is it for one day?
Was kostet es pro Tag?
vass kostet ess pro tahk

Is there a mileage charge?
Wird ein Preis pro Kilometer erhoben?
veert ine price pro kilomayter airhohben

When do I have to return it?
Wann muß ich es wieder zurückbringen?
van mooss ish ess veeder tsoor<u>oo</u>kbring-en

Can we rent a baby/child seat (car seat)
Können wir einen Baby/Kindersitz mieten?
k<u>ur</u>nnen veer ine-nen baibee/kindairzits meeten?

Where is the nearest gas station?
Wo ist die nächste Tankstelle?
vo ist dee n<u>ay</u>kstuh t<u>a</u>nkshtelluh

How do I get to Fechenheim/Steinstraße?
Wie komme ich nach Fechenheim/zur Steinstraße?
vee k<u>o</u>mmuh ish nahκH f<u>e</u>shenhime/tsoor sht<u>i</u>ne-shtrahssuh

Is this the road to Munich?
Ist das die Straße nach München?
ist dass dee shtr<u>ah</u>ssuh nahκH m<u>oo</u>nshen

Which is the quickest way to Central Station?
Was ist der schnellste Weg zum Hauptbahnhof?
vass ist dair shn<u>e</u>lstuh vayk tsoom h<u>ow</u>pt-bahnhof

---

DIRECTIONS YOU MAY BE GIVEN

an der nächsten Ausfahrt	at the next junction
an der nächsten Kreuzung	at the next intersection
erste Straße rechts	first on the right
geradeaus	straight ahead
links	on the left
links abbiegen	turn left
rechts	on the right
rechts abbiegen	turn right
vorbei an …	past the …
zweite Straße links	second on the left

THINGS YOU'LL SEE

Ausfahrt	exit
Autowäsche	car wash
Benzin	gas
bleifrei	leadfree
Bremsflüssigkeit	brake fluid
Einfahrt	entrance
Geschwindigkeits- beschränkung	speed limit
LKW	oversized vehicle
Luftdruck	air pressure
Motor abstellen	turn off engine
Münztank	coin-operated pump
Normal(benzin)	regular (gas)
Öl	oil
Parkhaus	multi-story parking lot
Parkplatz	parking lot
Parkschein entnehmen	take a ticket
PKW	private car
Reifendruck	tire pressure
Reparaturwerkstatt	garage, repairs
Schritt fahren	drive at walking speed
Super	super (gas)
Tankstelle	gas station
unverbleit	unleaded
verbleit	leaded
Waschstraße	car wash
Wasser	water
Zapfsäule	gas pump

THINGS YOU'LL HEAR

Kann ich bitte Ihren Führerschein sehen?
May I see your driver's license, please?

TRAVELING AROUND

AIR TRAVEL

In addition to an excellent domestic network, air services connect the following German cities with many US and UK destinations: Berlin, Bremen, Cologne (**Köln**), Bonn, Düsseldorf, Frankfurt am Main, Hamburg, Hanover, Leipzig, Munich (**München**), Nuremberg (**Nürnberg**), and Stuttgart.

TRAIN TRAVEL

The German Federal Railways or **DB** (**Deutsche Bundesbahn**) are outstanding for their punctuality and general efficiency. International trains connect Germany with most parts of Europe, while fast, regular Inter-City and express trains link the larger German towns and cities. The main types of train are:

TEE	Trans European Express
IC	Inter-City
D	Express
E(Eilzug)	Semi-fast train
Personenzug	Local train—stopping at every station

A supplement, or **Zuschlag** (*tsooshlahk*), is payable for all trips by **TEE** and **IC** trains, and on some **D** trains for trips under 50km.

LOCAL TRANSPORTATION, BOAT TRAVEL

There are good bus and tram systems in all German towns and cities. One-way tickets can be bought from a ticket machine located by the bus or tram stop, or sometimes from the driver. It is usually cheaper to buy a multi-trip ticket from a ticket machine. If you need to change buses or trams en route it is not necessary to buy another ticket. In some cities you will also have to stamp your ticket in a ticket-stamping machine situated on board the bus or tram—you will have to do this if you have bought a multi-trip ticket.

Some of the larger cities such as Hamburg, Munich, Berlin, Frankfurt, Cologne, and Nuremberg have a subway system or **U-Bahn** (_oobahn_) and some cities also have a fast, local train system or **S-Bahn** (_ess-bahn_). Zone systems also operate in major cities, a flat fare applying in each zone with the fare increasing according to the number of zones crossed. Tickets can be obtained from automatic ticket machines, most of which give change.

A number of rural bus services are also run by the German Federal Railways and Federal Post. Mail buses are yellow, while those belonging to the Federal Railways are red.

A more leisurely way of traveling in Germany, especially during the summer months, is on one of the steamer services operated on the major rivers such as the Rhine (**der Rhein**), Moselle (**die Mosel**, _mohzel_), and Danube (**die Donau**, _dohnow_), and on Lake Constance (**der Bodensee**, _bohdenzay_), the Bavarian lakes, and the Berlin lakes.

Taxis

Taxis are normally found at a taxi stand or can be ordered by telephone. It is not customary in Germany to hail a taxi on the street.

Useful Words and Phrases

adult	der Erwachsene	_airvaksenuh_
airport	der Flughafen	_flook-hahfen_
airport bus	der Flughafenbus	_flook-hahfenbooss_
aisle seat	der Sitz am Gang	_sits am gang_
baggage claim	die Gepäckausgabe	_gupek-owssgahbuh_
boarding pass	die Bordkarte	_bort-kartuh_
boat	das Schiff	_shiff_
bus	der Bus	_booss_
bus station	der Busbahnhof	_boossbahnhohf_
bus stop	die Bushaltestelle	_booss-haltuh-shtel-luh_

car *(train)*	der Wagen	v*ah*gen
carry-on luggage	das Handgepäck	h*a*nt-gup*e*k
check-in desk	der Abfertigungs-schalter	*a*pfairtigoongs-shalter
child	das Kind	kint
compartment	das Abteil	apt*ile*
connection	die Verbindung	fairbindoong
cruise	die Kreuzfahrt	kr*oy*ts-fart
customs	der Zoll	tsoll
departure lounge	die Abflughalle	*a*pfl*oo*k-halluh
dining car	der Speisewagen	shp*y*zuh-vahgen
domestic	Inland-	inl*a*nt-
emergency exit *(on plane)*	der Notausgang	n*oh*t-owssgang
	der Notausstieg	n*oh*t-owss-shteek
entrance	der Eingang	*ine*-gang
exit	der Ausgang	*ow*ssgang
fare	der Fahrpreis	f*a*rprice
ferry	die Fähre	f*ay*ruh
first class	die erste Klasse	*airstuh* kl*a*ssuh
flight	der Flug	fl*oo*k
flight number	die Flugnummer	fl*oo*knoommer
gate	der Flugsteig	fl*oo*k-shtike
international	international	internats-yon*ah*l
lost and found	das Fundbüro	f*oo*nt-b*œ*ro
luggage cart	der Gepäckkarren	gup*e*k-karren
luggage room	die Gepäck-aufbewahrung	gup*e*k-owfbuva-roong
transit system map	der Netzplan	n*e*tsplahn
nonsmoking	Nichtraucher	n*i*shtrowкнer
number 5 bus	der Bus Nr. 5	b*oo*ss n*oo*mmer f*œœ*nf
one-way ticket	die einfache	*ine*-f*a*кнuh
passport	der Paß	pas
platform	der Bahnsteig	b*ah*n-shtike
railroad	die Eisenbahn	*ize*-en-bahn

reservations office	der Fahrkarten-schalter	*farkarten-shalter*
reserved seat	der reservierte Platz	*rezerveertuh plats*
round-trip ticket	die Rückfahrkarte	*rookfarkartuh*
seat	der Platz	*plats*
second class	die zweite Klasse	*tsvytuh klassuh*
sleeper	der Schlafwagen	*shlahf-vahgen*
smoking	Raucher	*rowKHer*
station	der Bahnhof	*bahnhof*
subway	die U-Bahn	*oobahn*
taxi	das Taxi	*taxi*
terminal	die Endstation	*ent-shtats-yohn*
ticket	die Fahrkarte	*farkartuh*
(air)	das Ticket	*'ticket'*
timetable	der Fahrplan	*farplahn*
train	der Zug	*tsook*
tram	die Straßenbahn	*shtrahssenbahn*
waiting room	der Wartesaal	*vartuh-zahl*
window seat	der Fensterplatz	*fensterplats*

AIR TRAVEL

I'd like a nonsmoking seat, please
Ich möchte gern einen Nichtraucherplatz
ish murshtuh gairn ine-en nisht-rowKHerplats

I'd like a window seat, please
Ich möchte gern einen Fensterplatz
ish murshtuh gairn ine-en fensterplats

How long will the flight be delayed?
Wie lange dauert die Verspätung?
vee lang-uh veert dowert dee fairshpehtoong

Which gate for the flight to …?
Von welchem Flugsteig fliegt die Maschine nach …?
fon velshem flook-shtike fleekt dee masheenuh nahKH

TRAIN, BUS, AND SUBWAY TRAVEL

When does the train/bus for Frankfurt leave?
Wann fährt der Zug/Bus nach Frankfurt ab?
van fairt dair tsook/booss nahKH frankfoort ap

When does the train/bus from Munich arrive?
Wann kommt der Zug/Bus aus München an?
van kommt dair tsook/booss owss moonshen an

When is the next train/bus to Nuremberg?
Wann fährt der nächste Zug/Bus nach Nürnberg?
van fairt dair naykstuh tsook/booss nahKH noornbairk

When is the first train/bus to Pforzheim?
Wann fährt der erste Zug/Bus nach Pforzheim?
van fairt dair airstuh tsook/booss nahKH pforts-hime

When is the last train/bus to Cologne?
Wann fährt der letzte Zug/Bus nach Köln?
van fayrt dair letstuh tsook/booss nahKH kurln

What is the fare to Heidelberg?
Was kostet die Fahrt nach Heidelberg?
vass kostet dee fart nahKH hydelbairk

Do I have to change?
Muß ich umsteigen?
mooss ish oomshtygen

Does the train/bus stop at Lüneburg?
Hält der Zug/Bus in Lüneburg?
helt dair tsook/booss in loonuh-boork

How long does it take to get to Dresden?
Wie lange dauert die Fahrt nach Dresden?
vee lang-uh dowert dee fart nahKH draysden

Where can I buy a ticket?
Wo kann ich eine Fahrkarte lösen?
vo kan ish ine-uh farkartuh lurzen

A one-way/round-trip ticket to Bremen, please
Eine einfache Fahrkarte/eine Rückfahrkarte nach Bremen, bitte
*ine-uh ine-faкнuh farkartuh/ine-uh rꝏckfarkartuh nahкн braymen
bittuh*

Could you help me get a ticket?
Könnten Sie mir bitte helfen, eine Fahrkarte zu lösen?
kurnten zee meer bittuh helfen ine-uh farkartuh tsoo lurzen

Do I have to pay a supplement?
Muß ich einen Zuschlag zahlen?
mooss ish ine-en tsooshlahk tsahlen

Do we have to pay for the children?
Müssen Kinder auch Eintritt bezahlen?
murssen kindair owкн ine-tritt betsahlen?

Is there a family ticket available?
Gibt es eine Familienkarte?
gipt as ine-nuh fahmeelee-ankahrte?

I'd like to reserve a seat
Ich möchte gern einen Platz reservieren
ish murshtuh gairn ine-en plats rezerveeren

Is this the right train/bus for Bonn?
Ist das der Zug/Bus nach Bonn?
ist dass dair tsook/booss nahкн bon

Is this the right platform for the Wiesbaden train?
Ist das das Gleis für den Zug nach Wiesbaden?
ist dass dass glice fꝏr dayn tsook nahкн veessbahden

Which platform for the Düsseldorf train?
Von welchem Gleis fährt der Zug nach Düsseldorf?
fon velshem glice fairt dair tsook nahкн dꝏsseldorf

Is the train/bus late?
Hat der Zug/Bus Verspätung?
hat dair tsook/booss fairshpaytoong

Could you help me with my luggage, please?
Könnten Sie mir bitte mit meinem Gepäck helfen?
kurnten zee meer bittuh mit mine-em gupek helfen

Is this a nonsmoking compartment?
Ist das ein Nichtraucherabteil?
ist dass ine nishtrowkher-aptile

Is this seat free?
Ist dieser Platz frei?
ist deezer plats fry

This seat is taken
Dieser Platz ist besetzt
deezer plats ist buzetst

I have reserved this seat
Ich habe eine Reservierung für diesen Platz
ish hahbuh ine-uh rezerveeroong foor deezen plats

May I open/close the window?
Kann ich das Fenster öffnen/schließen?
kan ish dass fenster urfnen/shleessen

When do we arrive in Saarbrücken?
Wann kommen wir in Saarbrücken an?
van kommen veer in zarbrooken an

What station is this?
Wo sind wir hier?
vo zint veer heer

Do we stop at Singen?
Halten wir in Singen?
halten veer in zing-en

Is there a dining car on this train?
Hat dieser Zug einen Speisewagen?
hat deezer tsook ine-en shpyzuh-vahgen

THINGS YOU'LL HEAR

Der nächste Zug fährt um neun Uhr dreißig
The next train leaves at 9:30

Umsteigen in Darmstadt
Change at Darmstadt

Sie müssen einen Zuschlag zahlen
You have to pay a supplement

Es sind keine Plätze mehr frei
There are no more seats available

Where is the nearest subway station?
Wo ist die nächste U-Bahn-Station?
vo ist dee naykstuh oobahn-shtats-yohn

Where is the bus station?
Wo ist der Busbahnhof?
vo ist dair boossbahnhohf

Which buses go to Baden-Baden?
Welche Busse fahren nach Baden-Baden?
velshuh boossuh faren nahKH bahden-bahden

How often do the buses to Travemünde run?
Wie oft fahren die Busse nach Travemünde?
vee oft faren dee boossuh nahKH trahvuh-moonduh

Will you let me know when we're there?
Sagen Sie mir bitte Bescheid, wenn wir da sind?
zahgen zee meer bittuh bushite ven veer da zint

Do I have to get off here?
Muß ich hier aussteigen?
mooss ish heer owss-shtygen

How do you get to Bad Homburg?
Wie komme ich am besten nach Bad Homburg?
*vee k*_o_*mmuh ish am b*_e_*sten nah*_KH_ *baht h*_o_*mboork*

I want to go to Hamelin
Ich möchte nach Hameln fahren
*ish m*_u_*rshtuh nah*_KH_ *h*_a_*hmeln f*_a_*ren*

Do you go near Wildbad?
Fahren Sie in die Nähe von Wildbad?
*f*_a_*ren zee in dee n*_ay_*-uh fon v*_i_*ltbaht*

TAXIS

To the airport, please
Zum Flughafen bitte
*tsoom fl*_oo_*khahfen b*_i_*ttuh*

How much will it cost?
Wieviel kostet das?
vee-feel kostet dass

Could you stop here?
Können Sie hier halten, bitte
*k*_u_*rnen zee heer h*_a_*lten b*_i_*ttuh*

Could you wait for a moment, then take me back?
Können Sie hier einen Moment warten, und mich dann wieder zurückfahren?
*k*_u_*rnen zee heer* _ine_*-en mom*_e_*nt v*_a_*rten oont mish dan v*_ee_*der tsoor*_ew_*kfaren*

THINGS YOU'LL SEE

Abfahrt	departure(s)
Abfertigung	check-in
Abflug	departure(s)
Ankunft	arrival(s)
Ausgang	departure, exit
Auskunft	information
Ausland	international
außer sonntags	except Sundays
Ausweis	pass
Bahnhofsmission	office providing help for travelers in difficulty
Bahnhofspolizei	railroad police
Bahnsteig	platform
Bahnsteigkarte	platform ticket
Behinderte	disabled persons
besetzt	occupied
bezahlen	to pay
bitte anschnallen	fasten seat belt
Damen	women
DB (Deutsche Bundesbahn)	German trains
Direktflug	direct flight
einchecken	to check in
einfache Fahrt	single trip
Einstieg nur mit Fahrausweis	obtain a ticket before boarding
Einstieg vorn/hinten	entrance at front/rear
einwerfen	to insert
Endstation	terminal
Entwerter	ticket stamping machine
Erwachsene	adults
Fahrausweis	ticket
Fahrer	driver
Fahrgäste	passengers

→

Fahrkarte	ticket
Fahrkartenautomat	ticket machine
Fahrkartenschalter	tickets, ticket office
Fahrplan	timetable
Fahrschein	ticket
Fahrscheinkauf vom Fahrer	buy your ticket from the driver
Fahrt	trip
Flug	flight
Flugdauer	flight time
Flughafenbus	airport bus
Flugplan	timetable
Flugsteig	gate
frei	vacant
Geldeinwurf	insert money here
Geldrückgabe	returned coins
Gepäckaufbewahrung	luggage storage
Gepäckausgabe	baggage claim
Gepäckschließfächer	luggage lockers
gesperrt	closed, no entry
Gleis	platform
Hafen	harbor
Hafenrundfahrt	boat trip round the harbor
hält nicht in …	does not stop in …
Haltestelle	stop
Hauptbahnhof (Hbf)	central station
Herren	men
hier einsteigen	enter here
Imbiß	snacks
Inland	domestic
kein Ausstieg	no exit
kein Einstieg	exit only, enter by other door
kein Zugang	no entry
Kinder	children
Kurzstrecke	short distance (with a lower fare)

→

Linie	line, airline
Linienflug	scheduled flight
Mehrfahrtenkarte	multi-trip ticket
Mißbrauch strafbar	penalty for misuse
Monatskarte	monthly ticket
Münzen	coins
Nah(Schnell)verkehrszug	local train
Netzkarte	travelcard
nicht hinauslehnen	do not lean out of the window
nicht rauchen	no smoking
Nichtraucher	nonsmokers
Notausgang	emergency exit
Notausstieg	emergency exit
Notbremse	emergency brake
nur werktags	weekdays only
Ortszeit	local time
Passagiere	passengers
passendes Fahrgeld	exact fare
Paßkontrolle	passport control
Platzkarte	seat reservation
Rauchen verboten	no smoking
Raucher	smokers
Reiseauskunft	travel information
reserviert	reserved
Sammelkarte	multi-trip ticket
samstags	on Saturdays
S-Bahn	local railroad system
Schlafwagen	sleeper
Schließfächer	luggage room
Sitzplätze	seats
sonn- und feiertags	on Sundays and national holidays
Speisewagen	dining car
Stehplätze	standing room
Strecke	route

→

Tageskarte	day ticket
U-Bahn	subway
U-Bahnhof	subway station
umsteigen	to change
Verspätung	delay
Wagen	car (train)
Wagenstandanzeiger	order of cars
Wartesaal	waiting room
Wechselstube	currency exchange
zahlen	to pay
Zeitungen/Zeitschriften	newspapers/magazines
Zoll	customs
zu den Zügen	to the trains
zuschlagpflichtig	supplement must be paid
Zwischenlandung	intermediate stop

THINGS YOU'LL HEAR

Haben Sie Gepäck?
Do you have any luggage?

Raucher oder Nichtraucher?
Smoking or nonsmoking?

Fenstersitz oder Sitz am Gang?
Window seat or aisle seat?

Kann ich bitte Ihren Paß/Ihr Ticket sehen?
May I see your passport/ticket, please?

Die Passagiere werden gebeten, sich zum Flugsteig 7 zu begeben
Passengers are requested to proceed to gate 7

Erster/letzter Aufruf für Flug 302 nach Chicago
First/last call for flight 302 to Chicago

→

Achtung!
Attention!

Bitte einsteigen
Board the train

Der Zug nach Lübeck hat Einfahrt nach Gleis 7
The train for Lübeck is approaching platform 7

Vorsicht bei der Einfahrt des Zuges
Please stand clear of the approaching train

Planmäßige Ankunft: 13 Uhr 50
Scheduled arrival: 13:50

Der Zug hält nicht in Brühl
The train does not stop in Brühl

Der Zug fährt sofort ab
The train is now leaving

Der Zug hat zehn Minuten Verspätung
The train is ten minutes late

Bitte von der Bahnsteigkante zurücktreten
Please stand clear of the edge of the platform

Einsteigen und Türen schließen
Board the train and close the doors

Die Fahrkarten bitte
Tickets, please

Noch jemand zugestiegen?
Any more tickets?

EATING OUT

In Germany you'll find as wide a range of restaurants as in any country, from the gourmet deluxe to the sausage and fries kiosk on the pavement. Fast food outlets, Chinese, Italian, and Greek restaurants will be familiar. Not so perhaps the **Balkangrill**, serving spicy dishes from the Balkan countries. If you want something typically German you could do a lot worse than try a small **Gasthaus** (*gast-howss*) or inn. Some dishes vary from region to region, but one shared characteristic you'll find is that German portions are not skimpy. Germans tend to eat a lot of meat; vegetarians might have to make a special request.

Ask for a small beer (**ein kleines Bier**, *ine kline-ess beer*) and you'll normally get a glass of about 0.2 liters. A large beer (**ein großes Bier**, *ine grohss-ess beer*) will normally be 0.4 or 0.5 liters, although in Bavaria you may well get a liter, which is known as **eine Maß** (*ine-uh mahss*). German beer is usually **Pils**. In some areas you might try **Alt**, which is a darker beer. German wine is either **süß** (*sœss*, "sweet"), **trocken** (*trocken*, "dry"), or, if you like it dry and a little sharper, **herb** (*hairp*). If you'd like to try a local wine, ask for **einen Wein aus dieser Gegend** (*ine-en vine owss deezer gaygent*).

If you're having a drink in a pub or bar you don't pay when ordering. Instead the bartender or barmaid will keep a tally of what you've bought, often checking it off on your beer mat. If you sit at a table, you can expect table service (for no extra charge). There are no restrictions on taking children into pubs.

USEFUL WORDS AND PHRASES

appetizer	die Vorspeise	*forshpyzuh*
beer	das Bier	*beer*
bottle	die Flasche	*flashuh*
bread	das Brot	*broht*
butter	die Butter	*booter*

café	das Café	*kaffay*
cake	der Kuchen	*kooкнen*
carafe	die Karaffe	*karaffuh*
check	die Rechnung	*reshnoong*
children's portion	der Kinderteller	*kinderteller*
coffee	der Kaffee	*kaffay*
cup	die Tasse	*tassuh*
dessert	das Dessert	*dessair*
fork	die Gabel	*gahbel*
glass	das Glas	*glahss*
half liter	der halbe Liter	*halbuh leeter*
knife	das Messer	*messer*
main course	das Hauptgericht	*howpt-gurisht*
menu	die Speisekarte	*shpyzuh-kartuh*
milk	die Milch	*milsh*
napkin	die Serviette	*zairvee-ettuh*
pepper	der Pfeffer	*pfeffer*
plate	der Teller	*teller*
receipt	die Quittung	*kvittoong*
restaurant	das Restaurant	*restorong*
salt	das Salz	*zalts*
sandwich	das belegte Brot	*bulayktuh broht*
snack	der Imbiß	*imbiss*
soup	die Suppe	*zooppuh*
spoon	der Löffel	*lurfel*
sugar	der Zucker	*tsooker*
table	der Tisch	*tish*
tea	der Tee	*tay*
teaspoon	der Teelöffel	*taylurfel*
tip	das Trinkgeld	*trinkgelt*
waiter	der Ober	*ohber*
waitress	die Bedienung	*budeenoong*
water	das Wasser	*vasser*
wine	der Wein	*vine*
wine list	die Weinkarte	*vine-kartuh*

A table for one/two/three, please
Einen Tisch für eine Person/zwei/drei Personen, bitte
ine-en tish f∞r ine-uh pairzohn/tsvy/dry pairzohnen bittuh

May I see the menu/wine list?
Könnte ich bitte die Speisekarte/Weinkarte haben?
kurntuh ish bittuh dee shpyzuh-kartuh/vine-kartuh hahben

What would you recommend?
Was könnten Sie empfehlen?
vass kurnten zee empfaylen

I'd like …
Ich hätte gern …
ish hettuh gairn

Just a cup of coffee, please
Nur eine Tasse Kaffee, bitte
noor ine-uh tassuh kaffay bittuh

I only want a snack
Ich möchte nur eine Kleinigkeit
ish murshtuh noor ine-uh kline-ishkite

Is there a fixed-price menu?
Gibt es ein Tagesgericht?
geept ess ine tahges-gurisht

A liter carafe of house red, please
Einen Liter roten Tafelwein, bitte
ine-en leeter rohten tahfel-vine bittuh

Do you have any vegetarian dishes?
Haben Sie vegetarische Gerichte?
hahben zee vegetarishuh gurishtuh

Could we have some water, please?
Könnten Sie uns ein Glas Wasser geben?
kurnten zee oonss ine glas vasser gayben

Two more beers, please
Noch zwei Bier, bitte
noкн tsvy beer bittuh

Do you do children's portions?
Gibt es auch Kinderteller?
geept ess owкн kinderteller

Is there a highchair/baby changing room?
Gibt es dort einen Hochstuhl/einen Wickelraum?
gipt as dohrt ine-nen hoкнshtuhl/ine-en vikkelrowm?

Waiter/Waitress!
Herr Ober!/Fräulein!
hair ohber/froyline

We didn't order this
Das haben wir nicht bestellt
dass hahben veer nisht bushtellt

I'm still waiting for my dessert
Ich warte noch auf mein Dessert
ish vahrtuh noкн owf mine dessair

May we have some more …?
Könnten wir noch etwas … haben?
kurnten veer noкн etvass … hahben

May I have a different knife/fork?
Kann ich bitte ein anderes Messer/eine andere Gabel haben?
kan ish bittuh ine anderess messer/ine-uh anderuh gahbel hahben

May we have the check, please?
Zahlen, bitte
tsahlen bittuh

Could I have a receipt, please?
Könnte ich bitte eine Quittung bekommen?
kurntuh ish bittuh ine-uh kvittoong bukommen

Can we pay separately?
Können wir getrennt bezahlen?
kurnen veer gutrennt butsahlen

The meal was very good, thank you
Es hat sehr gut geschmeckt, vielen Dank
es hat zair goot gushmeckt feelen dank

THINGS YOU'LL HEAR

Guten Appetit!
Enjoy your meal!

Was möchten Sie trinken?
What would you like to drink?

Hat es Ihnen geschmeckt?
Did you enjoy your meal?

THINGS YOU'LL SEE

Bedienung inbegriffen	service included
Bierkeller	beer cellar
Eiscafé	ice-cream parlor (also serves coffee and liqueurs)
Gasthaus	inn, small restaurant, tavern (sometimes with accommodations)
Gaststätte	inn, small restaurant, tavern
Ratskeller	restaurant and bar close to town hall
Schnellimbiß	take out, snack bar (no seating)
Speisekarte	menu
Tageskarte	menu of the day
Weinstube	wine bar (traditional style)
Wirtshaus	tavern

MENU GUIDE

Aal	eel
Aalsuppe	eel soup
am Spieß	on the spit
Ananas	pineapple
Äpfel	apples
Apfel im Schlafrock	baked apple in puff pastry
Apfelkompott	stewed apples
Apfelmus	apple purée
Apfelsaft	apple juice
Apfelsinen	oranges
Apfelstrudel	apple strudel
Apfeltasche	apple turnover
Apfelwein	cider
Aprikosen	apricots
Arme Ritter	French toast
Artischocken	artichokes
Aspik	aspic
Auberginen	eggplant
Auflauf	(baked) pudding or omelette
Aufschnitt	sliced cold meats, cold cuts
Austern	oysters
Backobst	dried fruit
Backpflaume	prune
Baiser	meringue
Balkansalat	cabbage and pepper salad
Bananen	bananas
Bandnudeln	ribbon noodles
Basilikum	basil
Bauernauflauf	bacon and potato omelette
Bauernfrühstück	bacon and potato omelette
Bauernomelett	bacon and potato omelette
Bechamelkartoffeln	sliced potatoes in creamy sauce
Bechamelsoße	creamy sauce with onions and ham
Bedienung	service
Beilagen	side dishes
Berliner	jelly doughnut
Bier	beer
Birnen	pears

Biskuit	sponge cake
Biskuitrolle	Swiss roll
Bismarckhering	filleted pickled herring
Blätterteig	puff pastry
blau	boiled
Blaukraut	red cabbage
Blumenkohl	cauliflower
Blumenkohlsuppe	cauliflower soup
blutig	rare
Blutwurst	black pudding
Bockwurst	large hot dog
Bohnen	beans
Bohneneintopf	bean stew
Bohnensalat	bean salad
Bohnensuppe	bean soup
Bouillon	clear soup
Bouletten	meatballs
Braten	roast meat
Bratensoße	gravy
Brathering	(pickled) fried herring (served cold)
Bratkartoffeln	fried potatoes
Bratwurst	grilled pork sausage
Brot	bread
Brötchen	roll
Brühwurst	large hot dog
Brust	breast
Bückling	smoked red herring
Bunte Platte	mixed platter
Burgundersoße	Burgundy wine sauce
Buttercremetorte	cream cake
Buttermilch	buttermilk
Champignons	mushrooms
Champignonsoße	mushroom sauce
Chinakohl	Chinese cabbage
Cordon bleu	veal cordon bleu
Currywurst mit Pommes frites	curried pork sausage with fries
Dampfnudeln	sweet yeast dumpling
Deutsches Beefsteak	ground patty, ground meat
Dicke Bohnen	fava beans
Dillsoße	dill sauce
durchgebraten	well-done

durchwachsen	with fat
durchwachsener Speck	fatty bacon
Eier	eggs
Eierauflauf	omelette
Eierkuchen	pancake
Eierpfannkuchen	pancake
Eierspeise	egg dish
eingelegt	pickled
Eintopf	stew
Eintopfgericht	stew
Eis	ice
Eisbecher	sundae
Eisbein	knuckles of pork
Eisschokolade	iced chocolate
Eissplittertorte	ice chip cake
Endiviensalat	endive salad
englisch	rare
Entenbraten	roast duck
entgrätet	boned
Erbsen	peas
Erbsensuppe	pea soup
Erdbeertorte	strawberry cake
Essig	vinegar
Falscher Hase	meat loaf
Fasan	pheasant
Feldsalat	lettuce
Fenchel	fennel
Fett	fat
Filet	fillet (steak)
Fisch	fish
Fischfilet	fish fillet
Fischfrikadellen	fishcakes
Fischstäbchen	fish sticks
Flädlesuppe	consommé with pancake strips
flambiert	flambéed
Fleischbrühe	bouillon
Fleischkäse	meat loaf
Fleischklößchen	meatball(s)
Fleischpastete	meat vol-au-vent
Fleischsalat	diced meat salad with mayonnaise
Fleischwurst	pork sausage

Fond	meat juices
Forelle	trout
Forelle blau	boiled trout
Forelle Müllerin (Art)	trout with butter and lemon (breaded)
Frikadelle	rissole
Frikassee	fricassee
fritiert	(deep-) fried
Froschschenkel	frog's legs
Fruchtsaft	fruit juice
Frühlingsrolle	spring roll
Gans	goose
Gänsebraten	roast goose
Gänseleber	goose liver
Gänseleberpastete	goose-liver pâté
garniert	garnished
Gebäck	pastries, cakes
gebacken	baked
gebraten	roast
gebunden	thickened
gedünstet	steamed
Geflügel	poultry
Geflügelleber	chicken liver
Geflügelleberragout	chicken liver ragoût
gefüllt	stuffed
gefüllte Kalbsbrust	veal roll
gekocht	boiled
gekochter Schinken	boiled ham
Gelee	gelatin
gemischter Salat	mixed salad
Gemüse	vegetable(s)
Gemüseplatte	assorted vegetables
Gemüsereis	rice with vegetables
Gemüsesalat	vegetable salad
Gemüsesuppe	vegetable soup
gepökelt	salted, pickled
geräuchert	smoked
Gericht	dish
geschmort	braised; stewed
Geschnetzeltes	strips of meat in thick sauce
Geselchtes	salted and smoked meat
gespickt	larded

Getränke	beverages
Gewürze	spices
Gewürzgurken	gherkins
Goldbarsch	type of perch
Götterspeise	gelatin
gratiniert	au gratin
Grieß	semolina
Grießklößchen	semolina dumplings
Grießpudding	semolina pudding
Grießsuppe	semolina soup
grüne Bohnen	green beans
grüne Nudeln	green pasta
grüner Aal	fresh eel
Grünkohl	(curly) kale
Gulasch	goulash
Gulaschsuppe	goulash soup
Gurkensalat	cucumber salad
Hackfleisch	ground meat
Hähnchen	chicken
Hähnchenkeule	chicken leg
Haifischflossensuppe	shark-fin soup
Hammelbraten	roast mutton
Hammelfleisch	mutton
Hammelkeule	leg of mutton
Hammelrücken	saddle of mutton
Hartkäse	hard cheese
Haschee	hash
Hasenkeule	haunch of hare
Hasenpfeffer	hare casserole
Hauptspeisen	main courses
Hausfrauenart	homemade style
Hausmacher (Art)	homemade style
Hecht	pike
Heidelbeeren	bilberries, blueberries
Heilbutt	halibut
Heringssalat	herring salad
Heringsstipp	herring salad
Heringstopf	pickled herrings in sauce
Herz	heart
Herzragout	heart ragoût
Himbeeren	raspberries

Himmel und Erde	potato and apple purée with blood sausage or liver sausage
Hirn	brains
Hirschbraten	roast venison
Hirschmedaillons	small venison fillets
Honig	honey
Honigkuchen	honey cake
Honigmelone	honeydew melon
Hoppelpoppel	bacon and potato omelette
Hüfte	haunch
Huhn	chicken
Hühnerbrühe	chicken broth
Hühnerfrikassee	chicken fricassee
Hühnersuppe	chicken soup
Hülsenfrüchte	peas and beans, legumes
Hummer	lobster
Jägerschnitzel	cutlet with mushrooms
Kabeljau	cod
Kaffee	coffee
Kaiserschmarren	sugared pancake with raisins
Kakao	cocoa
Kalbfleisch	veal
Kalbsbraten	roast veal
Kalbsbries	sweetbread
Kalbsfrikassee	veal fricassee
Kalbshaxe	leg of veal
Kalbsmedaillons	small veal fillets
Kalbsnierenbraten	roast veal with kidney
Kalbsschnitzel	veal cutlet
kalte Platte	cold meal
kalter Braten	cold roast meat
kaltes Büfett	cold buffet
Kaltschale	cold sweet soup made from fruit
Kaninchen	rabbit
Kaninchenbraten	roast rabbit
Kapern	capers
Karamelpudding	caramel pudding
Karotten	carrots
Karpfen	carp
Kartoffelbrei	potato purée
Kartoffelklöße	potato dumplings

Kartoffelknödel	potato dumplings
Kartoffeln	potatoes
Kartoffelpuffer	potato fritters
Kartoffelpüree	potato purée
Kartoffelsalat	potato salad
Kartoffelsuppe	potato soup
Käse	cheese
Käse-Sahne-Torte	cream cheesecake
Käsegebäck	cheese snacks
Käsekuchen	cheesecake
Käseplatte	selection of cheeses
Käsesalat	cheese salad
Käsesoße	cheese sauce
Käsespätzle	homemade noodles with cheese
Kasseler Rippenspeer	salted rib of pork
Kasserolle	casserole
Kassler	smoked and braised pork chop
Kastanien	chestnuts
Katenrauchwurst	smoked sausage
Keule	leg, haunch
Kieler Sprotten	smoked sprats
Kirschen	cherries
klare Brühe	clear soup
Klößchensuppe	clear soup with dumplings
Klöße	dumplings
Knäckebrot	crispbread
Knacker	hot dog(s)
Knackwurst	hot dog
Knoblauch	garlic
Knoblauchbrot	garlic bread
Knochen	bone
Knochenschinken	ham on the bone
Knödel	dumplings
Kognak	brandy
Kohl	cabbage
Kohl und Pinkel	cabbage, potatoes, sausage, and smoked meat
Kohlrabi	kohlrabi (type of cabbage)
Kohlrouladen	stuffed cabbage leaves
Kompott	stewed fruit
Konfitüre	jam

Königinpastete	chicken vol-au-vent
Königsberger Klopse	meatballs in caper sauce
Königskuchen	type of fruit cake
Kopfsalat	lettuce
Kotelett	chop
Krabben	shrimp, prawns
Krabbencocktail	shrimp cocktail
Kraftbrühe	beef consommé
Kräuter	herbs
Kräuterbutter	herb butter
Kräuterkäse	cheese flavored with herbs
Kräuterquark	curd cheese with herbs
Kräutersoße	herb sauce
Kräutertee	herbal tea
Krautsalat	coleslaw
Krautwickel	stuffed cabbage leaves
Krebs	crab
Kresse	cress
Kroketten	croquettes
Kruste	crust
Kuchen	cake
Kürbis	pumpkin
Labskaus	meat, fish, and potato stew
Lachs	salmon
Lachsersatz	sliced and salted pollack (fish)
Lachsforelle	sea trout
Lachsschinken	smoked rolled fillet of ham
Lamm	lamb
Lammrücken	saddle of lamb
Langusten	crayfish
Lauch	leek
Leber	liver
Leberkäse	baked pork and beef loaf
Leberklöße	liver dumplings
Leberknödel	liver dumplings
Leberpastete	liver pâté
Leberwurst	liver pâté
Lebkuchen	type of gingerbread, often chocolate-covered
Leipziger Allerlei	mixed vegetables
Likör	liqueur

Limonade	lemonade
Linseneintopf	lentil stew
Linsensuppe	lentil soup
mager	lean
Majoran	marjoram
Makrele	mackerel
Makronen	macaroons
Mandeln	almonds
mariniert	marinaded, pickled
Markklößchen	marrow dumplings
Marmelade	jam
Marmorkuchen	marble cake
Maronen	sweet chestnuts
Matjes(hering)	young herring
Medaillons	small fillets
Meeresfische	seafish
Meeresfrüchte	seafood
Meerrettich	horseradish
Meerrettichsoße	horseradish sauce
Mehlspeise	sweet dish made with flour, milk, butter, and eggs
Melone	melon
Miesmuscheln	mussels
Milch	milk
Milchmixgetränk	milkshake
Milchreis	rice pudding
Mineralwasser	(sparkling) mineral water
Mohnkuchen	poppyseed cake
Möhren	carrots
Mohrrüben	carrots
Most	fruit wine
Mus	purée
Muscheln	mussels
Muskat(nuß)	nutmeg
MWSt = Mehrwertsteuer	VAT
nach Art des Hauses	of the house
nach Hausfrauenart	homemade
Nachspeisen	desserts
Nachtisch	dessert
Napfkuchen	ring-shaped poundcake
natürlich	natural

Nieren	kidneys
Nudeln	pasta
Nudelsalat	noodle salad
Nudelsuppe	noodle soup
Nüsse	nuts
Obstsalat	fruit salad
Ochsenschwanzsuppe	oxtail soup
Öl	oil
Oliven	olives
Olivenöl	olive oil
Omelett	omelette
Orangen	oranges
Orangensaft	orange juice
Palatschinken	stuffed pancakes
paniert	with breadcrumbs
Paprika	peppers
Paprikasalat	pepper salad
Paprikaschoten	peppers
Paradiesäpfel	tomatoes
Parmesankäse	parmesan cheese
Pastete	vol-au-vent
Pellkartoffeln	potatoes boiled in their skin
Petersilie	parsley
Petersilienkartoffeln	potatoes with parsley
Pfannkuchen	pancake(s)
Pfeffer	pepper
Pfifferlinge	chanterelles
Pfirsiche	peaches
Pflaumen	plums
Pflaumenkuchen	plum tart
Pflaumenmus	plum jam
Pichelsteiner Topf	vegetable stew with diced beef
pikant	spicy
Pikkolo	quarter bottle of champagne
Pilze	mushrooms
Pilzsoße	mushroom sauce
Pilzsuppe	mushroom soup
Platte	selection
pochiert	poached
Pökelfleisch	salted meat
Pommes frites	french fries

Porree	leek
Potthast	braised beef with sauce
Poularde	young chicken
Preiselbeeren	cranberries
Preßkopf	headcheese
Prinzeßbohnen	unsliced runner beans
Pumpernickel	black rye bread
Püree	(potato) purée
püriert	puréed
Putenschenkel	turkey leg
Puter	turkey
Quark	curd cheese
Quarkspeise	curd cheese dish
Radieschen	radishes
Rahm	(sour) cream
Räucheraal	smoked eel
Räucherhering	kipper, smoked herring
Räucherlachs	smoked salmon
Räucherspeck	smoked bacon
Rauchfleisch	smoked meat
Rehbraten	roast venison
Rehgulasch	venison goulash
Rehkeule	haunch of venison
Rehrücken	saddle of venison
Reibekuchen	potato waffles
Reis	rice
Reisauflauf	rice pudding
Reisbrei	creamed rice
Reisrand	with rice
Reissalat	rice salad
Remoulade	remoulade—mayonnaise flavored with herbs, mustard, and capers
Renke	whitefish
Rettich	radish
Rhabarber	rhubarb
Rheinischer Sauerbraten	braised beef
Rinderbraten	pot roast
Rinderfilet	fillet steak
Rinderrouladen	stuffed beef rolls
Rinderzunge	ox tongue
Rindfleisch	beef

Rindfleischsalat	beef salad
Rindfleischsuppe	beef broth
Rippchen	spareribs
Risi-Pisi	rice and peas
Risotto	risotto
roh	raw
Rohkostplatte	selection of salads
Rollmops	rolled-up pickled herring, rollmops
rosa	rare to medium
Rosenkohl	Brussels sprouts
Rosinen	raisins
Rostbraten	roast
Rostbratwurst	barbecued sausage
Rösti	fried potatoes and onions
Röstkartoffeln	fried potatoes
Rotbarsch	type of perch
Rote Bete	beet
rote Grütze	red fruit jelly
Rotkohl	red cabbage
Rotkraut	red cabbage
Rotwein	red wine
Rührei mit Speck	scrambled egg with bacon
Rühreier	scrambled eggs
Rumpsteak	rump steak
Russische Eier	eggs and mayonnaise
Sahne	cream
Sahnesoße	cream sauce
Sahnetorte	cream gâteau
Salate	salads
Salatplatte	selection of salads
Salatsoße	salad dressing
Salz	salt
Salzburger Nockerln	sweet soufflés
Salzheringe	salted herrings
Salzkartoffeln	boiled potatoes
Salzkruste	salty crusted skin
Sandkuchen	type of Madeira cake
sauer	sour
Sauerbraten	marinaded pot roast
Sauerkraut	white cabbage, finely chopped and pickled
Sauerrahm	sour cream

MENU GUIDE

Schaschlik	(shish-) kebab
Schattenmorellen	morello cherries
Schellfisch	haddock
Schildkrötensuppe	real turtle soup
Schillerlocken	smoked haddock rolls
Schinken	ham
Schinkenröllchen	rolled ham
Schinkenwurst	ham sausage
Schlachtplatte	selection of fresh sausages
Schlagsahne	whipped cream
Schlei	tench (fish)
Schmorbraten	pot roast
Schnecken	snails
Schnittlauch	chives
Schnitzel	breaded cutlet
Schokolade	chocolate
Scholle	plaice, flounder
Schulterstück	slice of shoulder
Schwarzbrot	brown rye bread
Schwarzwälder Kirschtorte	Black Forest cherry gâteau
Schwarzwurzeln	salsify
Schweinebauch	belly of pork
Schweinebraten	roast pork
Schweinefilet	fillet of pork
Schweinefleisch	pork
Schweinekotelett	pork chop
Schweineleber	pig's liver
Schweinerippe	cured pork chop
Schweinerollbraten	rolled roast of pork
Schweineschmorbraten	roast pork
Schweineschnitzel	pork fillet
Schweinshaxe	knuckle of pork
Seelachs	pollack (fish)
Seezunge	sole
Sekt	sparkling wine, champagne
Sellerie	celeriac
Selleriesalat	celeriac salad
Semmel	bread roll
Semmelknödel	bread dumplings
Senf	mustard
Senfsahnesoße	mustard and cream sauce

Senfsoße	mustard sauce
Serbisches Reisfleisch	diced pork, onions, tomatoes, and rice
Soleier	pickled eggs
Soße	sauce, gravy
Soufflé	soufflé
Spanferkel	suckling pig
Spargel	asparagus
Spargelcremesuppe	cream of asparagus soup
Spätzle	homemade noodles
Speck	fatty bacon
Speckknödel	bacon dumplings
Specksoße	bacon sauce
Speisekarte	menu
Spezialität des Hauses	specialty
Spiegeleier	fried eggs
Spießbraten	joint roasted on a spit
Spinat	spinach
Spitzkohl	white cabbage
Sprotten	sprats (herring)
Sprudel(wasser)	mineral water
Stachelbeeren	gooseberries
Stangen(weiß)brot	French bread
Steak	steak
Steinbutt	turbot
Steinpilze	type of mushroom
Stollen	type of fruit loaf
Strammer Max	ham and fried egg on bread
Streuselkuchen	cake with crumble topping
Sülze	headcheese
Suppen	soups
Suppengrün	mixed herbs and vegetables (used in soup)
süß	sweet
süß-sauer	sweet-and-sour
Süßspeisen	sweet dishes
Süßwasserfische	freshwater fish
Szegediner Gulasch	goulash with pickled cabbage
Tafelwasser	(uncarbonated) mineral water
Tafelwein	table wine
Tagesgericht	dish of the day
Tageskarte	menu of the day
Tagessuppe	soup of the day

Tatar	steak tartare
Taube	pigeon
Tee	tea
Teigmantel	pastry shell
Thunfisch	tuna
Tintenfisch	squid
Tomaten	tomatoes
Tomatensalat	tomato salad
Tomatensuppe	tomato soup
Törtchen	tart(s)
Torte	gâteau
Truthahn	turkey
überbacken	au gratin
Ungarischer Gulasch	Hungarian goulash
ungebraten	not fried
Vanille	vanilla
Vanillesoße	vanilla sauce
verlorene Eier	poached eggs
Vollkornbrot	dark whole grain bread
vom Grill	grilled
vom Kalb	veal
vom Rind	beef
vom Rost	grilled
vom Schwein	pork
Vorspeisen	hors d'oeuvres, appetizers
Waffeln	waffles
Waldorfsalat	salad with celery, apples, and walnuts
Wasser	water
Wassermelone	watermelon
Weichkäse	soft cheese
Weinbergschnecken	snails
Weinbrand	brandy
Weincreme	pudding with wine
Weinschaumcreme	creamed pudding with wine
Weinsoße	wine sauce
Weintrauben	grapes
Weißbier	carbonated light-colored beer made with wheat
Weißbrot	white bread
Weißkohl	white cabbage
Weißkraut	white cabbage

Weißwein	white wine
Weißwurst	veal sausage
Weizenbier	carbonated light-colored beer made with wheat
Wiener Schnitzel	veal in breadcrumbs
Wild	game
Wildschweinkeule	haunch of wild boar
Wildschweinsteak	wild boar steak
Windbeutel	cream puff
Wirsing	savoy cabbage
Wurst	sausage
Würstchen	hot dog(s)
Wurstplatte	selection of sausages
Wurstsalat	sausage salad
Wurstsülze	sausage headcheese
würzig	spicy
Zander	pike, perch (fish)
Zigeunerschnitzel	veal with peppers and relishes
Zitrone	lemon
Zitronencreme	lemon cream
Zucchini	zucchini
Zucker	sugar
Zuckererbsen	snow peas
Zunge	tongue
Zungenragout	tongue ragoût
Zutaten	ingredients
Zwiebeln	onions
Zwiebelringe	onion rings
Zwiebelsuppe	onion soup
Zwiebeltorte	onion tart
Zwischengerichte	entrées

STORES AND SERVICES

This chapter covers all kinds of shopping needs and services, and to start with you'll find some general phrases that can be used in lots of different places, many of which are listed below. After the general phrases come some more specific requests and sentences to use when you've found what you need, be it food, clothing, repairs, film-developing, or a haircut. Don't forget to refer to the mini-dictionary for items you may be looking for.

Stores in Germany are generally open from 9 AM to 6:30 PM, with some department stores and supermarkets staying open until 8:30 or 9 PM on Thursdays. On Saturdays stores normally close at 2 PM, except for the first Saturday of each month, when most remain open until 6 PM.

USEFUL WORDS AND PHRASES

antiques store	der Antiquitäten-laden	*antikvitayten-lahden*
audio equipment	die Phonoartikel	*fono-arteekel*
bakery	der Bäcker	*becker*
bookstore	die Buchhandlung	*booKHhantloong*
butcher's	der Metzger, der Fleischer	*metsger, flysher*
buy	kaufen	*kowfen*
camera store	der Fotoladen	*fotolahden*
camping equipment	die Campingartikel	*kempingarteekel*
candy store	der Süßwarenladen	*sαssvaren-lahden*
cash register	die Kasse	*kasse*
china	das Porzellan	*portsellahn*
cost	kosten	*kosten*
craft store	der Kunstgewerbe-laden	*Koonstguverbe-lahden*
department store	das Kaufhaus	*kowfhowss*

dry cleaner's	die chemische Reinigung	*shaymishuh rynigoong*
electrical goods store	der Elektroladen	*elektrolahden*
expensive	teuer	*toyer*
fish market	das Fischgeschäft	*fish-gusheft*
florist's	das Blumengeschäft	*bloomen-gusheft*
food store	das Lebensmittelgeschäft	*laybensmittel-gusheft*
fruit	das Obst	*ohpst*
gift store	der Geschenkladen	*gushenk-lahden*
grocer's	das Lebensmittelgeschäft	*laybensmittel-gusheft*
hair salon	der Friseur	*frizur*
hardware store	das Haushaltswarengeschäft	*howss-halts-varen-gusheft*
(for supplies)	die Eisenwarenhandlung	*ize-en-varen-hantloong*
inexpensive	billig	*billish*
jeweler's	der Juwelierladen	*yooveleer-lahden*
large department store	der Großmarkt	*grohssmarkt*
Laundromat	der Waschsalon	*vash-salong*
market	der Markt	*markt*
menswear	die Herrenbekleidung	*hairren-buklydoong*
newsstand	der Zeitungsladen	*tsytoongs-lahden*
optician's	der Optiker	*optiker*
pastry shop	die Konditorei	*konditor-ry*
produce market	die Gemüsehandlung	*gumoozuh-hantloong*
receipt	die Quittung	*kvittoong*
record store	das Schallplattengeschäft	*shallplatten-gusheft*
sale	der Schlußverkauf	*shlooss-fairkowf*
shoe repairer's	der Schuhmacher	*shoomaкнer*
shoe store	das Schuhgeschäft	*shoo-gusheft*

shopping bag	die (Trage)tasche	*(trahguh-)tashuh*
souvenir store	der Souvenirladen	*zooveneerlahden*
sports equipment	die Sportartikel	*shportarteekel*
sportswear	die Sportkleidung	*shport-klydoong*
stationery store	die Schreibwaren- handlung	*shryp-varen- hantloong*
store	der Laden, das Geschäft	*lahden, gusheft*
supermarket	der Supermarkt	*zoopermarkt*
tailor	der Schneider	*shnyder*
tobacco shop	der Tabakwarenladen	*tabakvaren-lahden*
toy store	die Spielwaren- handlung	*shpeelvaren- hantloong*
travel agent's	das Reisebüro	*ryzuhbooro*
vegetables	das Gemüse	*gumoozuh*
wine seller	die Weinhandlung	*vine-hantloong*
women's wear	die Damen- bekleidung	*dahmen-buklydoong*

Excuse me, where is/are ...? *(in a supermarket)*
Entschuldigung, wo finde ich ...?
ent-shooldigoong vo finduh ish

Where is there a ... (store)?
Wo gibt es ein Geschäft für ...?
vo geept ess ine gusheft foor

Where is the ... department?
Wo ist die ...-Abteilung?
vo ist dee ...-aptyloong

Where is the main shopping area?
Wo ist das Einkaufsviertel?
vo ist dass ine-kowfs-feertel

Is there a market here?
Gibt es hier einen Markt?
geept ess heer ine-en markt

I'd like …
Ich hätte gern …
ish hettuh gairn

Do you have …?
Haben Sie …?
hahben zee

How much is this?
Was kostet das?
vass kostet dass

Where do I pay?
Wo ist die Kasse?
vo ist dee kassuh

Do you take credit cards?
Akzeptieren Sie Kreditkarten?
aktsepteeren zee kredeetkarten

I think perhaps you've shortchanged me
Könnte es sein, daß Sie mir zu wenig herausgegeben haben
kurntuh ess zine dass zee meer tsoo vaynish hairowss-gugayben hahben

May I have a receipt?
Kann ich eine Quittung bekommen?
kan ish ine-uh kvittoong bukommen

May I have a bag, please?
Haben Sie eine Tragetasche, bitte?
hahben zee ine-uh trahguh-tashuh bittuh

I'm just looking
Ich sehe mich nur um
ish zay-uh mish noor oom

I'll come back later
Ich komme später wieder
ish kommuh shpayter veeder

Do you have any more of these?
Haben Sie noch mehr davon?
hahben zee nokh mair dafon

Do you have anything less expensive?
Haben Sie etwas Billigeres?
hahben zee etvass billigeress

Do you have anything larger/smaller?
Haben Sie etwas Größeres/Kleineres?
hahben zee etvass grursseress/kline-eress

May I try it/them on?
Kann ich es/sie anprobieren?
kan ish ess/zee anprobeeren

Does it come in other colors?
Gibt es das auch in anderen Farben?
geept es dass owkh in anderen farben

Could you gift wrap it for me?
Könnten Sie es mir als Geschenk einpacken?
kurnten zee ess meer alss gushenk ine-packen

I'd like to exchange this, it's defective
Ich möchte dies umtauschen, es ist defekt
ish murshtuh deess oomtowshen ess ist dayfekt

I'm afraid I don't have the receipt
Ich habe leider die Quittung nicht
ish hahbuh lyder dee kvittoong nisht

May I have a refund?
Kann ich mein Geld zurückbekommen?
kan ish mine gelt tsoorwk-bukommen

My camera isn't working
Meine Kamera funktioniert nicht
mine-uh kamera foonkts-yoneert nisht

I want a roll of 36-exposure color film, 100 ISO
Ich hätte gern einen Farbfilm für 36 Aufnahmen, 100 ISO
ish hettuh gairn ine-en farpfilm foor zex-oont-dryssish owfnah-men, hoondert ee-ess-oh

I'd like this film processed
Ich möchte diesen Film entwickeln lassen
ish murshtuh deezen film entvickeln lassen

Matte/glossy prints
Abzüge in matt/Hochglanz
aptsooguh in mat/hohкнglants

One-hour service, please
Ein-Stunden-Service, bitte
ine-shtoonden-service bittuh

Where can I get this fixed?
Wo kann ich das reparieren lassen?
vo kan ish dass repareeren lassen

(clothes)
Wo kann ich das ausbessern lassen?
vo kan ish dass owssbessern lassen

Can you fix this?
Können Sie das reparieren?
kurnen zee dass repareeren?

(clothes)
Können Sie das ausbessern?
kurnen zee dass owssbessern

I'd like this skirt/these pants dry-cleaned
Ich möchte diesen Rock/diese Hose reinigen lassen
ish murshtuh deezen rok/deezuh hohzuh rynigen lassen

When will it/will they be ready?
Wann ist es/sind sie fertig?
van ist ess/zint zee fairtish

85

I'd like some change for the washing machine/tumble dryer
Ich hätte gern Kleingeld für die Waschmaschine/den Trockner
ish hettuh gairn kline-gelt fœr dee vash-masheenuh/dayn trockner

Can you help me work the machine, please?
Können Sie mir helfen, die Maschine zu bedienen?
kurnen zee meer helfen dee masheenuh tsoo budeenen

I'd like to make an appointment
Ich hätte gern einen Termin
ish hettuh gairn ine-en tairmeen

I want a cut and blow-dry
Schneiden und fönen, bitte
shnyden oont furnen bittuh

With conditioner
Mit Pflegespülung
mit pflayguh-shpœloong

No conditioner, thanks
Keine Pflegespülung, danke
kine-uh pflayguh-shpœloong dankuh

Just a trim, please
Nur etwas nachschneiden, bitte
noor etvass nahκн-shnyden bittuh

A bit more off here, please
Hier bitte etwas kürzer
heer bittuh etvass kœrtser

Not too much off!
Nicht zu kurz!
nisht tsoo koorts

When does the market open?
Wann macht der Markt auf?
van maκнт dair markt owf

Is there one today in a town nearby?
Gibt es heute einen in einer Stadt in der Nähe?
geept ess hoytuh ine-en in ine-er shtat in dair nay-uh

What's the price per kilo?
Was kostet es pro Kilo?
vass kostet ess pro keelo

Could you write that down, please?
Könnten Sie mir das bitte aufschreiben?
kurnten zee meer dass bittuh owfshryben

That's very expensive!
Das ist aber sehr teuer!
dass ist ahber zair toyer

That's fine. I'll take it
In Ordnung. Ich nehme es
in ortnoong ish naymuh ess

I'll have a piece of that cheese
Ich hätte gern ein Stück von dem Käse
ish hettuh gairn ine sht∞k fon daym kayzuh

About 250/500 grams
Etwa 250/500 Gramm
etva tsvy-hoondert-f∞nftsish/f∞nf-hoondert gram

A kilo/half a kilo of apples, please
Ein Kilo/Pfund Äpfel, bitte
ine keelo/pfoont epfel bittuh

A quarter of a kilo of ham, please
Ein halbes Pfund gekochten Schinken, bitte
ine halbess pfoont gukoкнten shinken bittuh

May I taste it?
Kann ich mal probieren?
kan ish mal probeeren

No, I don't like the taste
Nein, das schmeckt mir nicht so gut
nine dass shmekt meer nisht zo goot

That's very nice, I'll take some
Das ist sehr lecker, davon nehme ich etwas
dass ist zair lecker dahfon naymuh ish etvass

It isn't what I wanted
Es ist nicht das, was ich wollte
ess ist nisht dass vass ish volltuh

THINGS YOU'LL SEE

Abteilung	department
Ausverkauf	sale
ausverkauft	sold out
Bäckerei	bakery
Blumen	flowers
Buchhandlung	bookstore
Büroartikel	office supplies
chemische Reinigung	dry cleaner's
Coiffeur	hairstylist
Damenkleidung	women's clothing
Damensalon	women's salon
Drogerie	chemist's
Fleischerei	butcher's
Friseur	barber's
Haarstudio	hairstyling studio
Heimwerkerbedarf	hardware store
herabgesetzt	reduced
Herrenkleidung	menswear
Herrensalon	men's hairstylist
Kasse	cash register
Kaufhaus	department store
Konditorei	pastry store

→

Lebensmittel	groceries
Metzgerei	butcher's
Mode	fashion
nicht berühren	do not touch
Obergeschoß	upper floor
Obst und Gemüse	fruit and vegetables
Pelze	furs
Preis	price
preiswert	bargain price, inexpensive
reduziert	reduced
Reisebüro	travel agent's
Schreibwaren	stationery
Schuhe	shoes
Schuhreparaturen	shoe repairs
Selbstbedienung	self-service
Sommerschlußverkauf	summer sale
Sonderangebot	special offer
Sonderpreis	special price
Spielwaren	toys
Spirituosen	liquor
Spitzenqualität	high quality
Süßwaren	candy store
Tabakwaren	tobacco shop
täglich frisch	fresh every day
Teppiche	carpets
Tiefgeschoß	lower floor, basement
Umtausch nur gegen Quittung	goods may not be exchanged without a receipt
vergriffen	unavailable, out of stock
vom Umtausch ausgeschlossen	may not be exchanged
Waschsalon	Laundromat
Winterschlußverkauf	winter sale
Zeitschriften	magazines
Zeitungen	newspapers

THINGS YOU'LL HEAR

Werden Sie schon bedient?
Are you being served?

Kann ich Ihnen helfen?
Can I help you?

Haben Sie es etwas kleiner?
Do you have anything smaller? (money)

Das haben wir gerade nicht vorrätig
I'm sorry we're out of stock

Das ist alles, was wir haben
This is all we have

Darf es sonst noch etwas sein?
Will there be anything else?

Darf es etwas mehr sein?
Is it okay if it's a bit over?

Wieviel hätten Sie gern?
How much would you like?

Wie möchten Sie es gern?
How would you like it?

Bezahlung mit Kreditkarte ist leider nicht möglich
I'm afraid it's not possible to pay by credit card

SPORTS

Whatever sport you choose and wherever you are in Germany you will not find a lack of facilities. The many lakes and rivers, as well as the North Sea and the Baltic Sea coasts, provide excellent opportunities for swimming, sailing, canoeing, fishing (permit required), sailboarding, etc., while an extensive network of well-marked trails makes Germany an ideal country for hiking. Bicycling is popular too, and bikes can be rented almost everywhere, including at many train stations.

Germany is known throughout the world as a center for winter sports, with about 300 resorts, mainly concentrated in the Alps, Black Forest, and Harz. In addition, many other areas have good facilities for cross-country skiing, while most of the larger towns have an ice rink, often open all year.

USEFUL WORDS AND PHRASES

Alps	die Alpen	_alpen_
athletics	Leichtathletik	_lysht-atlaytik_
badminton	Badminton	_'badminton'_
ball	der Ball	_bal_
beginners' slope	der Idiotenhügel	_idee-ohten-hoogel_
bicycle	das Fahrrad	_far-raht_
bicycle path	der Radweg	_rahtvayk_
binding (_ski_)	die Bindung	_bindoong_
canoe	das Kanu	_kahnoo_
canoeing	Kanufahren	_kahnoofaren_
cross-country skiing	Langlauf	_langlowf_
current	die Strömung	_shtrurmoong_
cycling	Radfahren	_rahtfaren_
dive	tauchen	_towKHen_
diving board	das Sprungbrett	_shproongbret_
downhill skiing	Abfahrtslauf	_apfartslowf_
fishing	Angeln	_ang-eln_
fishing rod	die Angelrute	_ang-el-rootuh_

flippers	die Schwimmflossen	*shvimflossen*
game	das Spiel	*shpeel*
goggles	die Taucherbrille	*towкнerbrilluh*
golf	Golf	*'golf*
golf course	der Golfplatz	*golfplats*
gymnastics	Gymnastik	*gɷmnastik*
hang-gliding	Drachenfliegen	*draкнenfleegen*
hiking	Bergwandern	*bairkvandern*
hockey	Hockey	*'hockey'*
hunting	die Jagd	*yahkt*
ice hockey	Eishockey	*ice-'hockey'*
jogging	Jogging	*'jogging'*
mast	der Mast	*mast*
mountaineering	Bergsteigen	*bairk-shtygen*
oars	die Ruder	*rooder*
oxygen bottle	die Sauerstoffflasche	*zowershtoff-flashuh*
pedal boat	das Tretboot	*traytboht*
piste	die Piste	*pistuh*
racket	der Schläger	*shlayger*
ride (*verb*)	reiten	*rite-en*
riding	Reiten	*rite-en*
riding hat	die Reitermütze	*rite-er-mɷtsuh*
rock climbing	Felsklettern	*felz-klettern*
row (*verb*)	rudern	*roodern*
rowboat	das Ruderboot	*rooderboht*
run (*verb*)	laufen	*lowfen*
saddle	der Sattel	*zattel*
sail (*noun*)	das Segel	*zaygel*
(*verb*)	segeln	*zaygeln*
sailboard	das Windsurfbrett	*vintsurf-bret*
sailing	Segeln	*zaygeln*
go sailing	segeln gehen	*zaygeln gayen*
skate (*verb*)	eislaufen	*ice-lowfen*
skates	die Schlittschuhe	*shlitt-shoo-uh*
skating rink	die Eislaufbahn	*ice-lowfbahn*
ski (*noun*)	der Ski	*shee*

ski (verb)	Ski fahren	*shee faren*
ski boots	die Skistiefel	*shee-shteefel*
skiing	Skilaufen	*sheelowfen*
ski lift	der Skilift	*sheelift*
skin diving	Sporttauchen	*shport-towкнen*
ski pass	der Skipaß	*sheepas*
ski poles	die Skistöcke	*shee-shturkuh*
ski tow	der Schlepplift	*shlep-lift*
ski trail	die Piste	*pistuh*
ski wax	das Skiwachs	*sheevax*
slalom	der Slalom	*slahlom*
sled	der Schlitten	*shlitten*
snorkel	der Schnorchel	*shnorshel*
soccer	Fußball	*foosbal*
soccer match	das Fußballspiel	*foosbal-shpeel*
sports center	das Sportzentrum	*shport-tsentroom*
stadium	das Stadion	*shtahdee-on*
surfboard	das Surfbrett	*surfbrett*
swim	schwimmen	*shvimmen*
swimming pool	das Schwimmbad	*shvimbaht*
swimsuit	der Badeanzug	*bahduh-antsook*
team	das Team	*'team'*
tennis	Tennis	*tennis*
tennis court	der Tennisplatz	*tennisplats*
tennis racket	der Tennisschläger	*tennis-shlayger*
toboggan	der Rodelschlitten	*rohdel-shlitten*
volleyball	Volleyball	*vollibal*
walk	wandern	*vandern*
walking	Wandern	*vandern*
water-ski	Wasserski fahren	*vasser-shee faren*
water-skiing	Wasserski	*vasser-shee*
water skis	die Wasserskier	*vasser-shee-er*
wet suit	der Tauchanzug	*towкнantsook*
go windsurfing	windsurfen gehen	*vintsurfen gayen*
winter sports	der Wintersport	*vintershport*
yacht	die Jacht	*yaкнt*

How do I get to the beach?
Wie komme ich zum Strand?
vee kommuh ish tsoom shtrant

How deep is the water here?
Wie tief ist das Wasser hier?
vee teef ist dass vasser heer

Is there an indoor/outdoor pool here?
Gibt es hier ein Hallenbad/Freibad?
geept ess heer ine hal-en-baht/frybaht

Is it safe to swim here?
Ist das Schwimmen hier sicher?
ist dass shvimmen heer zisher

Can I fish here?
Kann man hier angeln?
kan man heer ang-eln

Do I need a license?
Braucht man eine Genehmigung?
browкнt man ine-uh gunaymigoong

Is there a golf course near here?
Gibt es in der Nähe einen Golfplatz?
geept ess in dair nay-uh ine-en golfplats

Do I have to be a member?
Muß man Mitglied sein?
mooss man mitgleet zine

I would like to rent a bicycle/some skis
Ich möchte ein Fahrrad/Skier leihen
ish murshtuh ine far-raht/shee-er ly-en

How much does it cost per hour/day?
Was kostet es pro Stunde/Tag?
vass kostet ess pro shtoonduh/tahk

I would like to take water-skiing lessons
Ich möchte gern Wasserskiunterricht nehmen
ish mur̲shtuh gairn va̲ssershee-oonterrisht na̲ymen

Where can I rent …?
Wo kann man … leihen?
vo kan man … ly̲-en

There's something wrong with this binding
Mit dieser Bindung stimmt etwas nicht
mit dee̲zer bi̲ndoong shti̲mmt e̲tvass nisht

How much is a weekly pass for the ski lift?
Was kostet ein Wochenpaß für den Skilift?
vass ko̲stet ine vo̲κнen-pas fʊr dayn she̲elift

What are the snow conditions like today?
Wie sind heute die Schneeverhältnisse?
vee zint ho̲ytuh dee shna̲y-fairheltnissuh

I'd like to try cross-country skiing
Ich möchte gern Langlauf probieren
ish mur̲shtuh gairn la̲nglowf probe̲eren

I haven't played this before
Das habe ich noch nie gespielt
das ha̲hbuh ish noκн nee gushpe̲elt

Let's go skating/swimming
Sollen wir eislaufen/schwimmen gehen?
zo̲llen veer i̲ce-lowfen/shvi̲mmen ga̲yen

What's the score?
Wie steht's?
vee shtayts

Who won?
Wer hat gewonnen?
vair hat guvo̲nnen

THINGS YOU'LL SEE

Angeln verboten	no fishing
Betreten der Eisfläche verboten	keep off the ice
Bootsverleih	boat rental
Eisstadion	ice rink
Fahrräder	bicycles
Fahrradverleih	bicycles for rent
Fahrradweg	bicycle path
Freibad	open-air swimming pool
Gefahr	danger
gefährliche Strömung	dangerous current
Hafen	port
Hafenpolizei	harbor police
Hallenbad	indoor swimming pool
Karten	tickets
Lawinengefahr	danger of avalanches
Radweg	bicycle path
Reitweg	bridle path
Rodelbahn	toboggan run
Schneeverwehung	snow drift
Schwimmen verboten	no swimming
Segelboote	sailing boats
Skipiste	ski slope
Sportzentrum	sports center
Sprungschanze	ski jump
Stadion	stadium
Strand	beach
Tauchen verboten	no diving
Tauwetter	thaw
Umkleidekabine	changing rooms
Wanderweg	trail
Wassersport	water sports
zum Skilift	to the ski lift
zu verleihen	for rent

POST OFFICES AND BANKS

Post offices can be identified by a yellow sign with the word
Post(amt) or the symbol of a post horn. Opening hours are
usually from 9 AM to 11:30 AM or midday, and from 2 or 3 PM
to 5:30 or 6 PM on Monday to Friday, with a 9 till 12 noon
Saturday opening. Mailboxes are yellow.

Most banks are open from 8:30 AM or 9 AM to 12:30 PM and
from 1:30 PM to 4 PM. On Thursdays they stay open until 6 PM.
Banks are closed on Saturdays and Sundays. Foreign currency
and traveler's checks can also be exchanged at some of the
larger hotels or at a foreign exchange office (**Wechselstube**).
When changing money in a bank, it is customary to make your
transaction at one desk and then go to a different desk, the
checkout, or **Kasse**, where your money will be paid out to you.

The German unit of currency is the **Mark**. One **Mark** is divided
into 100 **Pfennige**. Coins come in denominations of 1, 2, 5,
10, and 50 Pfennige and 1, 2, and 5 Marks. Bills are available
in 5, 10, 20, 50, 100, 200, 500, and 1,000 Mark denominations.
Prices are also shown in Euros now and Germans can hold
their bank account in Euros.

Credit cards are not that widely used in Germany, so don't be
surprised if a store or a train station declines to accept
payment by credit card.

USEFUL WORDS AND PHRASES

airmail	Luftpost	*looftposst*
ATM	der Geldautomat	*gelt-owtom-aht*
bank	die Bank	*bank*
bill/banknote	der Geldschein	*gelt-shine*
cash	das Bargeld	*bargelt*
change	wechseln	*vexeln*
check	der Scheck	*shek*
checkbook	das Scheckbuch	*shekbookH*
collection	die Leerung	*layroong*

counter	der Schalter	*sh*<u>a</u>*lter*
credit card	die Kreditkarte	*kre*<u>dee</u>*t-kartuh*
customs form	das Zollformular	*ts*<u>o</u>*ll-formoolar*
delivery	die Zustellung	*ts*<u>oo</u>*-shtelloong*
deposit (*noun*)	die Einzahlung	<u>*ine*</u>*-tsahloong*
(*verb*)	einzahlen	<u>*ine*</u>*-tsahlen*
dollar	der dollar	*doll*<u>a</u>*h*
exchange rate	der Wechselkurs	*v*<u>e</u>*xel-koors*
fax (*noun*)	das Fax	*fax*
(*verb: document*)	faxen	*f*<u>a</u>*xen*
form	das Formular	*formool*<u>a</u>*r*
general delivery	postlagernde	*p*<u>o</u>*sst-lahgernduh*
international	die Auslands-	<u>*ow*</u>*ss-lants-*
money order	überanweisung	<u>*ö*</u>*ber-anvyzoong*
letter	der Brief	*breef*
letter carrier	der Briefträger	*breef-trayger*
mail	die Post	*posst*
mailbox	der Briefkasten	*breefkasten*
money order	die Postanweisung	*p*<u>o</u>*sst-anvyzoong*
package/parcel	das Paket	*pak*<u>ay</u>*t*
post	die Post	*posst*
postage rates	das Porto	*p*<u>o</u>*rto*
postal order	die Geldanweisung	*g*<u>e</u>*lt-anvyzoong*
postcard	die Ansichtskarte	<u>*a*</u>*nzishts-kartuh*
post office	das Postamt	*p*<u>o</u>*sst-amt*
registered letter	das Einschreiben	<u>*ine*</u>*-shryben*
stamp	die Briefmarke	*breef-markuh*
surface mail	Post auf dem	*p*<u>o</u>*sst owf daym*
	Landweg	*l*<u>a</u>*ntvayk*
traveler's check	der Reisescheck	*ryzuh-shek*
withdraw	abheben	<u>*a*</u>*p-hayben*
withdrawal	die Abhebung	<u>*a*</u>*p-hayboong*
zip code	die Postleitzahl	*p*<u>o</u>*sstlite-tsahl*

How much is a letter/postcard to ...?
Was ist das Porto für einen Brief/eine Postkarte nach ...?
vass ist dass porto foor ine-en breef/ine-uh posstkartuh nahкн

I would like three one-Mark stamps
Ich hätte gern drei Briefmarken zu einer Mark
ish hettuh gairn dry breef-marken tsoo ine-er mark

I want to register this letter
Ich möchte diesen Brief als Einschreiben senden
ish murshtuh deezen breef alss ine-shryben zenden

I want to send this package to ...
Ich möchte dieses Paket nach ... senden
ish murshtuh deezes pakayt nahкн ... zenden

How long does the mail to ... take?
Wie lange ist die Post nach ... unterwegs?
vee languh ist dee posst nahкн ... oontervayks

Where can I mail this?
Wo kann ich das aufgeben?
vo kan ish dass owfgayben

Is there any mail for me?
Ist Post für mich da?
ist posst foor mish da

I'd like to send a fax
Ich möchte ein Fax schicken
ish murshtuh ine fax shicken

This is to go airmail
Ich möchte das per Luftpost senden
ish murshtuh dass per looftposst zenden

I'd like to change this into marks
Ich möchte das gern in D-Mark wechseln
ish murshtuh dass gairn in day-mark vexeln

Can I cash these traveler's checks?
Kann ich diese Reiseschecks einlösen?
kan ish deezuh ryzuh-sheks ine-lurzen

What is the exchange rate for the dollar?
Wie steht der Kurs für den dollar?
vee shtayt dair koors foor deen dollah

Can I draw cash using this credit card?
Kann ich mit dieser Kreditkarte Geld abheben?
kan ish mit deezer kredeet-kartuh gelt ap-hayben

I'd like it in 50 Mark bills
Ich möchte es gern in 50-Mark-Scheinen
ish murshtuh ess gairn in foonftsish-mark-shine-en

Could you give me smaller bills?
Könnten Sie es mir in kleineren Scheinen geben?
kurnten zee ess meer in kline-eren shine-en gayben

THINGS YOU'LL SEE

Absender	sender
ausfüllen	fill in
ausländische Währungen	foreign currency
Auslandsporto	overseas postage
Auszahlungen	withdrawals, cashier
Brief	letter
Briefmarken	stamps
Bundespost	Federal Post Office
Drucksachen	printed matter
Einschreibsendungen	registered mail
Einzahlungen	deposits
Empfänger	addressee
Gebühren	charges
Geldautomat	ATM
Geldwechsel	currency exchange

→

geöffnet	open
geschlossen	closed
Hausnummer	number
Inlandsporto	domestic postage
Kasse	cashier
Luftpostsendungen	airmail
nächste Leerung	next collection
Öffnungszeiten	opening hours
Ort	town, place
Päckchen	small packages
Paket	packages
Paketannahme	packages counter
Porto	postage
Postamt	post office
Postanweisungen	money orders
Postkarte	postcard
postlagernde Sendungen	general delivery
Postleitzahl	zip code
Postwertzeichen in kleinen Mengen	stamps in small quantities
Schalter	counter
Sparkasse	savings bank
Telefonzelle	telephone booth
Wechselkurs	exchange rate
Wechselstube	foreign exchange office

YOU MAY HEAR

Sie bekommen Ihr Geld an der Kasse
You'll get your money from the cashier

COMMUNICATIONS

Telephones: Telephone booths in Germany are yellow.
International calls can be made only from boxes that show a
green disk with the word **Ausland** or **International**. To call a
number in the US, dial 001 followed by the area code and
subscriber's number. Phonecards can be bought from post offices.

The tones you'll hear when telephoning in Germany are:

Dial tone: same as in US
Ringing: long high-pitched tone
Busy: rapid beeps
Unobtainable: voice says **Kein Anschluß unter dieser
                    Nummer**, and you'll hear three short
                    pips of ascending pitch.

In Germany, telephone numbers are read out in pairs of
numbers, for example, 302106 is said **dreißig, einundzwanzig,
null sechs** ("thirty, twenty-one, zero six"). It will, of course, also
be perfectly comprehensible to say a number as individual digits.

USEFUL WORDS AND PHRASES

call (*noun*)	der Anruf	*anroof*
(*verb*)	anrufen	*anroofen*
cardphone	das Kartentelefon	*karten-telefohn*
code	die Vorwahl	*forvahl*
collect call	das R-Gespräch	*air-gushpraysh*
crossed line	die Fehlverbindung	*fayl-fairbindoong*
dial	wählen	*vaylen*
dial tone	das Amtszeichen	*amts-tsyshen*
directory	die Auskunft	*owsskoonft*
assistance		
email address	die E-mail Adresse	*ee-mail adressuh*
extension	der Nebenanschluß	*nayben-anshlooss*
fax machine	das Faxgerät	*faxgerayt*

102

international call	das Auslands-gespräch	owsslants-gush-praysh
internet	das Internet	'internet'
mobile phone	das Mobiltelefon	mohbeeltelefohn
number	die Nummer	noommer
operator	die Vermittlung	fairmittloong
payphone	das Münztelefon	moonts-telefohn
phone book	das Telefonbuch	telefohn-bookн
phonecard	die Telefonkarte	telefohn-kartuh
receiver	der Hörer	hur-er
telephone	das Telefon	telefohn
telephone booth	die Telefonzelle	telefohn-tselluh
website	die Webseite	'website'
wrong number	die falsche Nummer	falshuh noommer

Where is the nearest phone booth?
Wo ist die nächste Telefonzelle?
vo ist dee naykstuh telefohn-tselluh

I would like the phone book for …
Ich hätte gern das Telefonbuch für …
ish hettuh gairn dass telefohn-bookн foor

Can I call abroad from here?
Kann man von hier ins Ausland anrufen?
кan man fon heer inss owsslant anroofen

I would like to make a collect call
Ich möchte ein R-Gespräch führen
ish murshtuh ine air-gushpraysh fooren

I would like a number in …
Ich hätte gern eine Nummer in …
ish hettuh gairn ine-uh noommer in

Could you give me an outside line?
Geben Sie mir bitte das Amt
gayben zee meer bittuh dass amt

How do I get an outside line?
Wie kann ich nach draußen telefonieren?
vee kan ish nahкн dr<u>ow</u>ssen telefon<u>ee</u>ren

Hello, this is … speaking
Hallo, hier spricht …
h<u>a</u>llo heer shprisht

Is that …?
Ist das …?
ist dass

Speaking
Am Apparat
am apar<u>a</u>ht

May I speak to …, please
Kann ich bitte … sprechen?
kan ish b<u>i</u>ttuh … shpr<u>e</u>shen

Extension …, please
Anschluß …, bitte
anshl<u>oo</u>ss … b<u>i</u>ttuh

Please tell him/her … called
Bitte sagen Sie ihm/ihr, daß … angerufen hat
b<u>i</u>ttuh z<u>a</u>hgen zee eem/eer dass … <u>a</u>nguroofen hat

Would you ask him/her to call me back, please
Sagen Sie ihm/ihr bitte, er/sie möchte mich zurückrufen
z<u>a</u>hgen zee eem/eer b<u>i</u>ttuh air/zee m<u>u</u>rshtuh mish tsoor<u>oow</u>k-r<u>oo</u>fen

Do you know where he/she is?
Wissen Sie, wo er/sie ist?
v<u>i</u>ssen zee vo air/zee ist

When will he/she be back?
Wann wird er/sie zurück sein?
van veert air/zee tsoor<u>oow</u>k zine

Could you leave him/her a message?
Können Sie ihm/ihr etwas ausrichten?
kurnen zee eem/eer etvass owssrishten

I'll call back later
Ich rufe später zurück
ish roofuh shpayter tsoorωk

Sorry, (I've got the) wrong number
Tut mir leid, ich habe mich verwählt
toot meer lite ish hahbuh mish fairvaylt

What's your fax number/email address?
Wie ist Ihre Faxnummer/E-mail Adresse?
vee isst eeruh faxnummer/ee-mail adressuh?

Did you get my fax/email?
Haben Sie mein Fax/meine E-mail erhalten?
hahben zee mine fax/mine-nuh ee-mail airhalten?

May I send a fax/email from here?
Kann ich von hier ein Fax/eine E-mail senden?
kan ish von hear ine fax/ine-nuh ee-mail zenden?

THE ALPHABET

a	*ah*	h	*hah*	o	*o*	v	*fow*
b	*bay*	i	*ee*	p	*pay*	w	*vay*
c	*tsay*	j	*yot*	q	*koo*	x	*ix*
d	*day*	k	*kah*	r	*air*	y	*ωpsilon*
e	*ay*	l	*el*	s	*ess*	z	*tset*
f	*ef*	m	*em*	t	*tay*		
g	*gay*	n	*en*	u	*oo*		

SPECIAL GERMAN CHARACTERS

ä	*eh*	ö	*ur*	ü	*ω*	ß	*ess-tset*

THINGS YOU'LL SEE

abnehmen	lift (the receiver)
Amerika	America
Apparat	telephone
Auskunft	(directory) assistance
Auslandsgespräche	international calls
außer Betrieb	out of order
besetzt	busy
defekt	out of order
Durchwahl	direct dialing
Einheit	unit
fasse dich kurz!	be brief!
Ferngespräche	long-distance calls
Fernsprecher	telephone
Feuer	fire
Feuerwehr	fire department
Gabel	hook
Gelbe Seiten	Yellow Pages
Geld einwerfen	insert money
Gespräch	call, conversation
Hörer	receiver
Karte ganz einschieben	push card right in
Mobiltelefon	mobile phone
Münzen	coins
Notruf	emergency call
Ortsgespräche	local calls
Rufnummer	number
Störungsstelle	faulty service
Telefonzelle	telephone booth
Vereinigten Staaten	United States
Vermittlung	operator
Vorwahl	code
wählen	to dial
warten	to wait
Webseite	website

THINGS YOU'LL HEAR

Am Apparat
Speaking

Wen möchten Sie sprechen?
Whom would you like to speak to?

Sie sind falsch verbunden
You've got the wrong number

Wer spricht bitte?
Who's speaking?

Welche Nummer haben Sie?
What is your number?

Tut mir leid, er ist nicht im Hause
Sorry, he's not here

Er ist um drei Uhr zurück
He'll be back at three o'clock

Bitte rufen Sie morgen nochmal an
Please call again tomorrow

Ich werde ihm/ihr sagen, daß Sie angerufen haben
I'll tell him/her you called

Kein Anschluß unter dieser Nummer
Number unavailable

Ich verbinde
I'll put you through

Bitte warten
Please hold

EMERGENCIES

In an emergency dial 110 for police or ambulance and 112 for fire. Drivers can get assistance from the **ADAC**, the German driving organization. If you break down on an autobahn, look for a small arrow on the marker posts at the side of the road: the arrow points in the direction of the nearest emergency telephone. Ask for the **Straßenwacht** (*shtrahssen-vaкнt*). Assistance will be free, but you will have to pay for parts.

USEFUL WORDS AND PHRASES

accident	der Unfall	*oonfal*
ambulance	der Krankenwagen	*kranken-vahgen*
assault *(verb)*	überfallen	*ωberfal-en*
breakdown	die Panne	*pannuh*
break down *(verb)*	eine Panne haben	*ine-uh pannuh hahben*
burglar	der Einbrecher	*ine-breкнer*
burglary	der Einbruch	*ine-brooкн*
crash	der Zusammenstoß	*tsoozammen-shtohss*
emergency	der Notfall	*nohtfal*
emergency room	die Unfallstation	*oonfal-stats-yohn*
fire	das Feuer	*foyer*
fire department	die Feuerwehr	*foyer-vayr*
flood	die Überschwemmung	*ωbershvemmoong*
injured	verletzt	*fairletst*
lose	verlieren	*fairleeren*
pickpocket	der Taschendieb	*tashendeep*
police	die Polizei	*poli-tsy*
police station	die Polizeiwache	*poli-tsy-vaкнuh*
rob	rauben	*rowben*
steal	stehlen	*shtaylen*
theft	der Diebstahl	*deep-shtahl*
thief	der Dieb	*deep*
tow	abschleppen	*ap-shleppen*
towing service	der Abschleppdienst	*ap-shlep-deenst*

Help!
Hilfe!
hilfuh

Look out!
Passen Sie auf!
pas-en zee owf

Stop!
Halt!
halt

This is an emergency!
Dies ist ein Notfall!
deess ist ine nohtfal

Get an ambulance!
Rufen Sie einen Krankenwagen!
roofen zee ine-en kranken-vahgen

Hurry up!
Beeilen Sie sich!
buh-ile-en zee zish

Please send an ambulance to …
Bitte schicken Sie einen Krankenwagen zu …
bittuh shicken zee ine-en kranken-vahgen tsoo

Please come to …
Bitte kommen Sie zu …
bittuh kommen zee tsoo

My address is …
Meine Adresse ist …
mine-uh adressuh ist

We've had a break-in
Bei uns ist eingebrochen worden
by oonss ist ine-gubroкнen vorden

There's a fire at …
Es brennt in …
ess brennt in

Someone's been injured/knocked down
Jemand ist verletzt/überfahren worden
yaymant ist fairletst/ooberfahren vorden

He's passed out
Er ist ohnmächtig
air ist ohnmeshtish

My passport/car has been stolen
Mein Paß/Auto ist gestohlen worden
mine pas/owto ist gushtohlen vorden

I've lost my traveler's checks/money
Ich habe meine Reiseschecks/geld verloren
ish hahbuh mine-uh ryzuh-sheks/gelt fairloren

I want to report a stolen credit card
Ich möchte den Diebstahl einer Kreditkarte melden
ish murshtuh dayn deep-shtahl ine-er kredeet-kartuh melden

It was stolen from my room
Es wurde aus meinem Zimmer gestohlen
ess voorduh owss mine-em tsimmer gushtohlen

I lost it in the park/on the train
Ich habe es im Park/im Zug verloren
ish hahbuh ess im park/im tsook fairlohren

My luggage is missing
Mein Gepäck ist verloren gegangen
mine gupek ist fairlohren gugang-en

Has my luggage turned up yet?
Ist mein Gepäck inzwischen aufgetaucht?
ist mine gupek intsvishen owfgutowкнt

The registration number is …
Mein amtliches Kennzeichen ist …
mine amtlishes ken-tsyshen ist

My car's been broken into
Mein Auto ist aufgebrochen worden
mine owto ist owfgubroкнen vorden

I've had a crash
Ich habe einen Unfall gehabt
ish hahbuh ine-en oonfal guhahpt

I've been mugged
Ich bin überfallen worden
ish bin ωberfal-en vorden

My son's missing
Mein Sohn ist verschwunden
mine zohn ist fairshvoonden

He has fair/brown hair
Er hat helles/braunes Haar
air hat helless/browness har

He's … years old
Er ist … Jahre alt
air ist … yaruh alt

I've locked myself out
Ich habe mich ausgesperrt
ish hahbuh mish owss-gushpairt

He's drowning
Er ist am Ertrinken
air ist am airtrinken

She can't swim
Sie kann nicht schwimmen
zee kan nisht shvimmen

THINGS YOU'LL SEE

Bergwacht	mountain rescue
Brand	fire
Erste Hilfe	first aid
Feuer	fire
Feuerlöscher	fire extinguisher
Krankenhaus	hospital
Lebensgefahr	danger of death
Nachtdienst	late night (pharmacy, etc.)
Notarzt	emergency doctor
Notausgang	emergency exit
Notfälle	emergencies
Notruf	emergency call
Notrufsäule	emergency telephone
Polizei	police
Polizeiwache	police station
Unfallrettung	ambulance, emergency service
Unfallstation	emergency room
Verkehrspolizei	traffic police

THINGS YOU'LL HEAR

Wo wohnen Sie?
What's your address?

Wo sind Sie?
Where are you?

Können Sie es/ihn beschreiben?
Can you describe it/him?

HEALTH

In Germany all pharmacies are independent private concerns.
There are no chain pharmacies. They exclusively sell
medicines and a small assortment of goods that have some
medicinal use. In every town you will find a pharmacy, or
Apotheke (*apotaykuh*), which is open all night or over the
weekend. Those that are closed will display a notice showing
which one is open, and the local newspaper will also advertise
the **dienstbereit** (*deenstburite*), or pharmacist on duty. You may
have to ring the night bell.

USEFUL WORDS AND PHRASES

ambulance	der Krankenwagen	*kranken-vahgen*
anemic	blutarm	*blootarm*
appendicitis	die Blinddarm-entzündung	*blintdarm-ent-ts∞ndoong*
aspirin	die Kopfschmerz-tablette	*kopfshmairts-tablettuh*
asthma	das Asthma	*astma*
backache	die Rückenschmerzen	*r∞ken-shmairtsen*
bandage	der Verband	*fairbant*
bite *(by dog)*	der Biß	*biss*
(by insect)	der Stich	*shtish*
bladder	die Blase	*blahzuh*
blister	die Blase	*blahzuh*
blood	das Blut	*bloot*
blood donor	der Blutspender	*bloot-shpender*
burn	die Verbrennung	*fairbrennoong*
cancer	der Krebs	*krayps*
chest	die Brust	*broost*
chickenpox	die Windpocken	*vintpocken*
cold	die Erkältung	*airkeltoong*
concussion	die Gehirn-erschütterung	*guheern-airsh∞teroong*

constipation	die Verstopfung	*fairsht<u>o</u>pfoong*
corn	das Hühnerauge	*h<u>oo</u>ner-owguh*
cough	der Husten	*h<u>oo</u>sten*
cut	der Schnitt	*shnit*
dentist	der Zahnarzt	*ts<u>ah</u>n-artst*
diabetes	die Zuckerkrankheit	*ts<u>oo</u>ker-krankhite*
diarrhea	der Durchfall	*d<u>oo</u>rshfal*
dizzy	schwindlig	*shv<u>i</u>ntlish*
doctor	der Arzt	*artst*
earache	die Ohrenschmerzen	*<u>o</u>ren-shmairtsen*
fever	das Fieber	*f<u>ee</u>ber*
filling	die Füllung	*f<u>ö</u>lloong*
first aid	die Erste Hilfe	*<u>ai</u>rstuh h<u>i</u>lfuh*
flu	die Grippe	*gr<u>i</u>ppuh*
fracture	der Bruch	*br<u>oo</u>KH*
German measles	die Röteln	*r<u>u</u>rteln*
glasses	die Brille	*br<u>i</u>lluh*
hay fever	der Heuschnupfen	*h<u>oy</u>shnoopfen*
headache	die Kopfschmerzen	*kopf-shm<u>ai</u>rtsen*
heart	das Herz	*hairts*
heart attack	der Herzinfarkt	*h<u>ai</u>rts-infarkt*
hemorrhage	die Blutung	*bl<u>oo</u>toong*
hepatitis	die Hepatitis	*'hepatitis'*
HIV positive	HIV positiv	*'HIV positive'*
hospital	das Krankenhaus	*kr<u>a</u>nken-howss*
ill	krank	*krank*
indigestion	die Magen-verstimmung	*m<u>ah</u>gen-fairsht<u>i</u>mmoong*
injection	die Spritze	*shpr<u>i</u>tsuh*
itch	das Jucken	*y<u>oo</u>cken*
kidney	die Niere	*n<u>ee</u>ruh*
lump	der Knoten	*k-n<u>oh</u>ten*
measles	die Masern	*m<u>ah</u>zern*
migraine	die Migräne	*migr<u>ay</u>nuh*
mumps	der Mumps	*moomps*

nausea	die Übelkeit	∞belkite
nurse *(female)*	die Kranken-schwester	kranken-shvester
nurse *(male)*	der Krankenpfleger	kranken-pflayger
operation	die Operation	operats-yohn
pain	der Schmerz	shmairts
penicillin	das Penizillin	penitsileen
pharmacy	die Apotheke	apotaykuh
plaster of Paris	der Gips	gips
pneumonia	die Lungen-entzündung	loongen-ents∞ndoong
pregnant	schwanger	shvanger
prescription	das Rezept	retsept
rheumatism	das Rheuma	royma
scald	die Verbrühung	fairbr∞-oong
scratch	der Kratzer	kratser
smallpox	die Pocken	pocken
sore throat	die Halsschmerzen	halss-shmairtsen
splinter	der Splitter	shplitter
sprain	die Verstauchung	fairshtowкноong
sting	der Stich	shtish
stomach	der Magen, der Bauch	mahgen, bowкн
temperature	das Fieber	feeber
tonsils	die Mandeln	mandeln
toothache	die Zahnschmerzen	tsahn-shmairtsen
travel sickness	die Reisekrankheit	ryzuh-krankhite
ulcer	das Geschwür	gushv∞r
vaccination	die Impfung	impfoong
vomit	erbrechen	airbreshen
whooping cough	der Keuchhusten	koysh-hoosten
wound	die Wunde	voonduh

I have a pain in …
Ich habe Schmerzen in …
ish hahbuh shmairtsen in

I do not feel well
Ich fühle mich nicht wohl
ish fooluh mish nisht vohl

I feel sick
Mir ist schlecht
meer ist shlesht

I feel dizzy
Mir ist ganz schwindlig
meer ist gants shvindlish

It hurts here
Es tut hier weh
ess toot heer vay

It's a sharp/dull pain
Es ist ein stechender/dumpfer Schmerz
ess ist ine shteshender/doompfer shmairts

It hurts all the time
Es tut ständig weh
ess toot shtendish vay

It only hurts now and then
Es tut nur ab und zu weh
ess toot noor ap oont tsoo vay

It hurts when you touch it
Es tut weh, wenn man draufdrückt
ess toot vay ven man drowfdrɷkt

It hurts more at night
Nachts ist es schlimmer
naкнts ist ess shlimmer

It stings/it aches/it itches
Es brennt/es tut weh/es juckt
ess brennt/ess toot vay/ess yookt

I have a temperature
Ich habe Fieber
ish hahbuh feeber

I'm … months pregnant
Ich bin im … Monat Schwanger
ish bin im … mohnat shvahngair

I need a prescription for …
Ich brauche ein Rezept für …
ish browкнuh ine retsept fΦr

I normally take …
Ich nehme normalerweise …
ish naymuh normahler-vyzuh

I'm allergic to …
Ich bin allergisch gegen …
ish bin alairgish gaygen

Have you got anything for …?
Haben Sie etwas gegen …?
hahben zee etvass gaygen

Can you take these if you're pregnant/breastfeeding?
Kann man diese während der Schwangerschaft/Stillzeit
 einnehmen?
kan man deezuh verent dair shvangershaft/shtiltsyte ine-naymen?

I have lost a filling
Ich habe eine Füllung verloren
ish hahbuh ine-uh fΦlloong fairloren

Will he/she be all right?
Wird er/sie sich wieder erholen?
veert air/zee zish veeder erhohlen

Will he/she need an operation?
Muß er/sie operiert werden?
mooss air/zee opereert vairden?

How is he/she?
Wie geht es ihm/ihr?
vee gayt ess eem/eer

THINGS YOU'LL SEE

Ambulanz	outpatients
Arzt	doctor
Augenarzt	ophthalmologist, optician
Augenoptiker	optician
Bereitschaftsdienst	doctor/pharmacist on duty
Blutdruck	blood pressure
dienstbereit	on duty
Erste Hilfe	first aid
Facharzt für …	specialist for …
Frauenarzt	gynecologist
Hals, Nasen, Ohren	ear, nose, and throat
Intensivstation	intensive care unit
Krankenhaus	hospital
Krankenkasse	medical insurance
Krankenwagen	ambulance
Medikament	medicine
Notarzt	emergency doctor
Notaufnahme	emergency room
Notfälle	emergencies
Praktischer Arzt	General Practitioner
Rezept	prescription
Sanitätsdienst	ambulance service
Medikament	medicine
Notarzt	emergency doctor
Notaufnahme	emergency room
Notfälle	emergencies
Praktischer Arzt	General Practitioner
Rezept	prescription
Sanitätsdienst	ambulance service
Sanitätsstelle	first aid center

Sprechstunde	surgery
Spritze	injection
Untersuchung	checkup
Termin	appointment
Wartezimmer	waiting room
Zahnarzt	dentist

THINGS YOU'LL HEAR

Nehmen Sie jeweils … Tabletten
Take … pills/tablets at a time

Mit Wasser
With water

Zum Zerkauen
Chew them

Einmal/zweimal/dreimal täglich
Once/twice/three times a day

Nur vor dem Schlafengehen
Only when you go to bed

Was nehmen Sie sonst?
What do you normally take?

Sie sollten besser zum Arzt gehen
I think you should see a doctor

Tut mir leid, das haben wir nicht
I'm sorry, we don't have that

Dafür brauchen Sie ein Rezept
You need a prescription for that

Auf nüchternen Magen
On an empty stomach

Der nächste bitte!
Next please!

CONVERSION TABLES

DISTANCES

A mile is 1.6km. To convert kilometers to miles, divide the km by 8 and multiply by 5. Convert miles to km by dividing the miles by 5 and multiplying by 8.

miles	0.62	1.24	1.86	2.43	3.11	3.73	4.35	6.21
miles *or* km	1	2	3	4	5	6	7	10
km	1.61	3.22	4.83	6.44	8.05	9.66	11.27	16.10

WEIGHTS

The kilogram is equivalent to 2lb 3oz. To convert kg to lbs, divide by 5 and multiply by 11. One ounce is about 28 grams, and 8 oz about 227 grams; 1lb is therefore about 454 grams.

lbs	2.20	4.41	6.61	8.82	11.02	13.23	19.84	22.04
lbs *or* kg	1	2	3	4	5	6	9	10
kg	0.45	0.91	1.36	1.81	2.27	2.72	4.08	4.53

TEMPERATURE

To convert Celsius degrees into Fahrenheit, the accurate method is to multiply the C° figure by 1.8 and add 32. Similarly, to convert F° to C°, subtract 32 from the F° figure and divide by 1.8.

C°	-10	0	5	10	20	30	36.9	40	100
F°	14	32	41	50	68	86	98.4	104	212

LIQUIDS

A liter is about 2.1 pints; a gallon is roughly 3.8 liters.

gals	0.27	0.53	1.33	2.65	5.31	7.96	13.26
gals *or* liters	1	2	5	10	20	30	50
liters	3.77	7.54	18.85	37.70	75.40	113.10	188.50

TIRE PRESSURES

lb/sq in	18	20	22	24	26	28	30	33
kg/sq cm	1.3	1.4	1.5	1.7	1.8	2.0	2.1	2.3

MINI-DICTIONARY

The word for "the" can be either **der**, **die**, or **das**, depending on whether a noun is masculine, feminine, or neuter. The plural is **die**. The corresponding words for "a" are **ein**, **eine**, or **ein**.

a ein, eine
about: about 16 etwa 16
accelerator das Gaspedal
accident der Unfall
accommodations die Unterkunft
ache der Schmerz
adaptor der Adapter
address die Adresse
adhesive der Klebstoff
admission charge der Eintrittspreis
after nach
aftershave das Rasierwasser
again nochmal
against gegen
agent der Vertreter
AIDS AIDS
air (noun) die Luft
air conditioning die Klimaanlage
aircraft das Flugzeug
airline die Fluglinie
airport der Flughafen
airport bus der Flughafenbus
aisle der Gang
alarm clock der Wecker
alcohol der Alkohol
all alle(s)
  all the streets alle Straßen
  that's all das ist alles
almost fast
alone allein
already schon
always immer
am: I am ich bin

ambulance der Krankenwagen
America Amerika
American (man) der Amerikaner
  (woman) die Amerikanerin
  (adj.) amerikanisch
and und
ankle der Knöchel
anorak der Anorak
another (different) ein anderer
  (one more) noch ein
  another room ein anderes Zimmer
  another coffee, please noch einen Kaffee, bitte
answering machine der Anrufbeantworter
antifreeze das Frostschutzmittel
antiques store das Antiquitätengeschäft
antiseptic das Antiseptikum
apartment die Wohnung
aperitif der Aperitif
appetite der Appetit
apple der Apfel
application form das Antragsformular
appointment der Termin
apricot die Aprikose
are: we/they are wir/sie sind
you are Sie sind
  (sing., familiar) du bist
arm der Arm
art die Kunst
art gallery die Kunstgalerie
artist der Künstler
  (female) die Künstlerin

as: as soon as possible so bald wie
    möglich
ashtray der Aschenbecher
asleep: he's asleep er schläft
aspirin die Kopfschmerztablette
at: at the post office auf der Post
    at the station am Bahnhof
    at night in der Nacht
    at 3 o'clock um 3 Uhr
ATM der Geldautomat
attractive attraktiv
aunt die Tante
Australia Australien
Australian *(man)* der Australier
    (woman) die Australierin
    (adj.) australisch
Austria Österreich
Austrian *(man)* der Österreicher
    (woman) die Österreicherin
    (adj.) österreichisch
auto-body shop die Werkstatt
automatic automatisch
away: is it far away? ist es weit von hier?
    go away! gehen Sie weg!
awful furchtbar
ax die Axt
axle die Achse

baby das Baby
baby carriage der Kinderwagen
baby wipes die Babytücher
back *(not front)* die Rückseite
    (body) der Rücken
    to come back zurückkommen
backpack der Rucksack
bacon der Speck
    bacon and eggs Eier mit Speck
bad schlecht
bag die Tasche
baggage claim die Gepäckausgabe
bait der Köder
bake backen
baker der Bäcker

balcony der Balkon
ball der Ball
ballpoint pen der Kugelschreiber
Baltic die Ostsee
banana die Banane
band *(musicians)* die Band
bandage der Verband
bangs *(hair)* der Pony
bank die Bank
banknote der (Geld)schein
bar *(drinks)* die Bar
    bar of chocolate
    die Tafel Schokolade
barber's der Herrenfriseur
bargain das Sonderangebot
basement das Untergeschoß
basin *(sink)* das Becken
basket der Korb
bath das Bad
    (tub) die Badewanne
    to take a bath ein Bad nehmen
bathroom das Badezimmer
battery die Batterie
Bavaria Bayern
beach der Strand
beans die Bohnen
beard der Bart
beautiful schön
because weil
bed das Bett
bed linen die Bettwäsche
bedroom das Schlafzimmer
beef das Rindfleisch
beer das Bier
before ... vor ...
beginner der Anfänger
beginners' slope der Idiotenhügel
behind ... hinter ...
beige beige
Belgian *(man)* der Belgier
    (woman) die Belgierin
    (adj.) belgisch
Belgium Belgien

bell (*church*) die Glocke
  (*door*) die Klingel
below ... unter ...
belt der Gürtel
beside neben
best bester
better besser
between ... zwischen ...
bicycle das Fahrrad
big groß
bikini der Bikini
bill die Rechnung
bird der Vogel
birthday der Geburtstag
  happy birthday! viel Glück zum
  Geburtstag!
birthday card die Geburtstagskarte
birthday present das
  Geburtstagsgeschenk
bite (*noun: by dog*) der Biß
  (*by insect*) der Stich
  (*verb*) beißen
  (*insect*) stechen
bitter bitter
black schwarz
blackberry die Brombeere
black currant die schwarze
  Johannisbeere
Black Forest der Schwarzwald
blanket die Decke
bleach (*noun*) das Bleichmittel
  (*verb: hair*) bleichen
blind (*cannot see*) blind
blinds die Jalousie
blister die Blase
blizzard der Schneesturm
blond (*adj.*) blond
  (*noun*) die Blondine
blood das Blut
blouse die Bluse
blue blau
boat das Schiff
  (*small*) das Boot

body der Körper
  (*corpse*) die Leiche
boil (*verb*) kochen
boiler der Boiler
bolt (*noun: on door*) der Riegel
  (*verb*) verriegeln
bone der Knochen
book (*noun*) das Buch
  (*verb*) buchen
bookstore die Buchhandlung
boot (*footwear*) der Stiefel
border die Grenze
boring langweilig
born: I was born in ...
  ich bin in ... geboren
both beide
  both of us wir beide
  both ... and ... sowohl ... als auch ...
bottle die Flasche
bottle opener der Flaschenöffner
bottom der Boden
  (*part of body*) der Hintern
  (*sea*) der Grund
bowl die Schüssel
box die Schachtel
box office die Kasse
boy der Junge
boyfriend der Freund
bra der Büstenhalter
bracelet das Armband
brake (*noun*) die Bremse
  (*verb*) bremsen
brandy der Weinbrand
bread das Brot
breakdown (*car*) die Panne
  (*nervous*) der Zusammenbruch
  I've had a breakdown ich habe eine
  Panne
breakfast das Frühstück
breathe atmen
bridge die Brücke
  (*game*) Bridge
briefcase die Aktentasche

Britain Großbritannien
British britisch
brochure die Broschüre
broiler der Grill
broken *(arm, etc.)* gebrochen
(*vase, etc.*) zerbrochen
(*machine, etc.*) kaputt
broken leg der Beinbruch
brooch die Brosche
brother der Bruder
brown braun
bruise der blaue Fleck
brush *(noun)* die Bürste
(*paint*) der Pinsel
(*verb: hair*) bürsten
(*floor*) kehren
Brussels Brüssel
bucket der Eimer
building das Gebäude
bumper die Stoßstange
burglar der Einbrecher
burn *(noun)* die Verbrennung
(*verb*) brennen
bus der Bus
business das Geschäft
it's none of your business das geht
Sie nichts an
busy *(occupied)* beschäftigt
(*bar, etc.*) voll
but aber
butcher's die Metzgerei
butter die Butter
button der Knopf
buy kaufen
by: by the window am Fenster
by Friday bis Freitag
by myself/himself allein

cabbage der Kohl
cabinet der Schrank
cable/satellite TV das Kabel-/
Satellitenfernsehen
cable car die Drahtseilbahn

café das Café
cake der Kuchen
calculator der Rechner
call: what's it called? wie heißt das?
to call *(to make a phone call)* anrufen
camcorder der Camcorder
camera die Kamera
campsite der Campingplatz
camshaft die Nockenwelle
can die Dose
can: can I have …?
kann ich … haben?
can you …? können Sie …?
Canada Kanada
Canadian *(man)* der Kanadier
(*woman*) die Kanadierin
(*adj.*) kanadisch
canal der Kanal
candle die Kerze
candy die Süßigkeit
canoe das Kanu
can opener der Dosenöffner
cap *(bottle)* der Verschluß
(*hat*) die Mütze
car das Auto
(*train*) der Wagen
carbonated sprudelnd
carburetor der Vergaser
card die Karte
cardigan die Strickjacke
careful sorgfältig
be careful! passen Sie auf!
caretaker der Hausmeister
carpet der Teppich
carrot die Möhre, die Karotte
car seat *(for a baby)* der Kindersitz
case *(suitcase)* der Koffer
cash *(noun)* das Bargeld
(*verb*) einlösen
to pay cash bar bezahlen
cassette die Kassette
cassette player der Kassetten-recorder
castle das Schloß, die Burg

cat die Katze
cathedral der Dom
cauliflower der Blumenkohl
cave die Höhle
cemetery der Friedhof
center *(middle)* die Mitte
central heating die Zentralheizung
certificate die Bescheinigung
chair der Stuhl
change *(noun: money)* das Kleingeld
  (verb: money) wechseln
  (clothes) sich umziehen
Channel der Kanal
check-in *(desk)* die Abfertigung
check in *(verb)* einchecken
cheers! prost!
cheese der Käse
check der Scheck
checkbook das Scheckheft
cherry die Kirsche
chess Schach
chest *(part of body)* die Brust
  (furniture) die Truhe
chest of drawers die Kommode
chewing gum der Kaugummi
chicken das Huhn
  (cooked) das Hähnchen
child das Kind
children die Kinder
china das Porzellan
chocolate die Schokolade
  box of chocolates die Schachtel
  Pralinen
chop *(food)* das Kotelett
  (verb: to cut) kleinschneiden
Chunnel der Kanaltunnel
church die Kirche
cigar die Zigarre
  (thin) das Zigarillo
cigarette die Zigarette
city die (Groß)stadt
city center das Stadtzentrum
class die Klasse

classical music die klassische
  Musik
clean *(adj.)* sauber
clear klar
clever klug
clock die Uhr
close *(near)* nah
  (stuffy) stickig
  (verb) schließen
closed geschlossen
clothes die Kleider
clubs *(cards)* Kreuz
clutch die Kupplung
coach *(train)* der Wagen
coat der Mantel
coat hanger der (Kleider)bügel
cockroach die Küchenschabe
coffee der Kaffee
coin die Münze
cold *(illness)* die Erkältung
  (adj.) kalt
  I have a cold ich bin erkältet
  I am cold mir ist kalt
collar der Kragen
collection *(stamps, etc.)* die Sammlung
  (postal) die Leerung
Cologne Köln
color die Farbe
color film der Farbfilm
comb *(noun)* der Kamm
come kommen
  I come from … ich komme aus …
  we came last week wir sind letzte
  Woche angekommen
  come here! kommen Sie her!
comforter die Steppdecke
compact disc die Compact-Disc
compartment das Abteil
complicated kompliziert
computer der Computer
concert das Konzert
conditioner *(hair)* die Haarspülung
condom das Kondom

conductor (*bus*) der Schaffner
  (*orchestra*) der Dirigent
congratulations! herzlichen
  Glückwunsch!
consulate das Konsulat
contact lenses die Kontaktlinsen
contraceptive das Verhütungsmittel
cook (*noun*) der Koch
  (*verb*) kochen
cookie das Plätzchen
cooking utensils das Koch-geschirr
cool kühl
cork der Korken
corkscrew der Korkenzieher
corner die Ecke
corridor der Korridor
cosmetics die Kosmetika
cost (*verb*) kosten
  what does it cost? was kostet das?
cotton die Baumwolle
cotton balls die watte
cough (*noun*) der Husten
  (*verb*) husten
cough drops die Halstabletten
country das Land
cousin (*male*) der Vetter
  (*female*) die Kusine
crab die Krabbe
cramp der Krampf
crayfish der Krebs
cream (*for cake, etc.*) die Sahne
  (*lotion*) die Creme
credit card die Kreditkarte
crowded überfüllt
cruise die Kreuzfahrt
crutches die Krücken
cry (*weep*) weinen
  (*shout*) rufen
cucumber die Gurke
cuff links die Manschettenknöpfe
cup die Tasse
curlers die Lockenwickler
curling iron der Lockenstab

curls die Locken
curry das Curry
curtain der Vorhang
Customs der Zoll
cut (*noun*) der Schnitt
  (*verb*) schneiden

dad der Vater
damp feucht
dance (*noun*) der Tanz
  (*verb*) tanzen
Dane (*man*) der Däne
  (*woman*) die Dänin
Danish dänisch
dangerous gefährlich
Danube die Donau
dark dunkel
daughter die Tochter
day der Tag
dead tot
deaf taub
dear (*person*) lieb
  (*expensive*) teuer
debit card die Scheckkarte
deck of cards das Kartenspiel
deep tief
delayed verspätet
deliberately absichtlich
Denmark Dänemark
dentist der Zahnarzt
dentures die Prothese
deny bestreiten
deodorant das Deodorant
department store das Kaufhaus
departure die Abfahrt
departure lounge die Abflughalle
develop (*film*) entwickeln
diamond (*jewel*) der Diamant
diamonds (*cards*) Karo
diaper die Windel
diarrhea der Durchfall
diary das Tagebuch
dictionary das Wörterbuch

die sterben
diesel der Diesel
different verschieden
  that's different!
  das ist etwas anderes!
  I'd like a different kind ich möchte
  gern eine andere Sorte
difficult schwierig
dining car der Speisewagen
dining room der Speiseraum
dirty schmutzig
disabled behindert
dish cloth das Geschirrtuch
dishwashing liquid das Spülmittel
disposable diapers die Einwegwindeln
distributor (*car*) der Autohändler
dive (*noun*) der Sprung
  (*verb*) tauchen
diving board das Sprungbrett
divorced geschieden
do tun
  how do you do? guten Tag
  (*on being introduced*) freut mich
dock der Kai
doctor der Arzt
document das Dokument
dog der Hund
doll die Puppe
dollar der Dollar
door die Tür
double room das Doppelzimmer
doughnut der Berliner
down herunter
  (*position*) unten
  down here hier unten
dress das Kleid
drink (*noun*) das Getränk
  (*verb*) trinken
  would you like a drink?
  möchten Sie etwas trinken?
drinking water das Trinkwasser
drive (*verb*) fahren
driver der Fahrer

driver's license der Führerschein
driving regulations die
  Straßenverkehrsordnung
drunk betrunken
dry trocken
dry cleaner's die (chemische) Reinigung
during während
dust cloth das Staubtuch
Dutch (*adj.*) holländisch
Dutchman der Holländer
Dutchwoman die Holländerin
duty-free zollfrei

each (*every*) jeder
  five marks each fünf Mark das Stück
ear das Ohr
early früh
earrings die Ohrringe
ears die Ohren
east der Osten
easy leicht
eat essen
egg das Ei
either: either of them einer von beiden
  either … or … entweder … oder …
elastic elastisch
elbow der Ellbogen
electric elektrisch
electricity der Strom
elevator der Fahrstuhl
else: something else etwas anderes
  someone else jemand anders
  somewhere else woanders
email die E-mail
email address die E-mail Adresse
embarrassing peinlich
embassy die Botschaft
embroidery die Stickerei
emerald der Smaragd
emergency der Notfall
emergency brake die Notbremse
emergency exit der Notausgang
empty leer

end das Ende
engaged *(couple)* verlobt
engine *(motor)* der Motor
England England
English *(adj.)* englisch
  (language) Englisch
Englishman der Engländer
Englishwoman die Engländerin
enlargement die Vergrößerung
enough genug
entertainment die Unterhaltung
entrance der Eingang
envelope der (Brief)umschlag
escalator die Rolltreppe
especially besonders
evening der Abend
every jeder
everyone jeder
everything alles
everywhere überall
example das Beispiel
  for example zum Beispiel
excellent ausgezeichnet
excess baggage das Mehrgepäck
exchange *(verb)* (um)tauschen
exchange rate der Wechselkurs
excursion der Ausflug
excuse me! Entschuldigung!
exit der Ausgang
expensive teuer
extension cord die Verlängerungsschnur
eye das Auge
  eyes die Augen

face das Gesicht
faint *(unclear)* blaß
  (verb) ohnmächtig werden
fair *(amusement park)* der Jahrmarkt
  (just) gerecht, fair
false teeth die Prothese
family die Familie
fan *(ventilator)* der Ventilator
  (enthusiast) der Fan

fan belt der Keilriemen
fantastic fantastisch
far weit
  how far is it? wie weit ist es?
fare der Fahrpreis
farm der Bauernhof
farmer der Bauer
fashion die Mode
fast schnell
fat *(person)* dick
  (on meat, etc.) das Fett
father der Vater
fax *(noun)* das Fax
  (verb: document) faxen
fax machine das Faxgerät
feel *(touch)* fühlen
  I feel hot mir ist heiß
  I feel like … ich möchte gern …
  I don't feel well
  mir ist nicht gut
feet die Füße
felt-tip pen der Filzstift
fence der Zaun
ferry die Fähre
fever das Fieber
fiancé der Verlobte
fiancée die Verlobte
field das Feld
fig die Feige
filling *(in tooth, cake)* die Füllung
  (in sandwich) der Belag
film der Film
filter der Filter
filter papers das Filterpapier
finger der Finger
fire das Feuer
fire extinguisher der Feuerlöscher
fireworks das Feuerwerk
first erster
first aid die Erste Hilfe
first floor der erste Stock
first name der Vorname
fish der Fisch

fishing das Angeln
  to go fishing Angeln gehen
fish market das Fischgeschäft
flag die Fahne
flash *(camera)* der Blitz
flashlight die Taschenlampe
flat *(level)* flach
flavor der Geschmack
flea der Floh
flight der Flug
flight attendant die Stewardess
flippers die (Schwimm)flossen
floor *(ground)* der Boden
  (story) der Stock
flour das Mehl
flower die Blume
flute die Flöte
fly *(insect)* die Fliege
  (verb) fliegen
fog der Nebel
folk music die Volksmusik
food das Essen
food poisoning die Lebensmittelvergiftung
foot der Fuß
for für
  for me für mich
  what for? wofür?
  for a week für eine Woche
foreigner der Ausländer
  (female) die Ausländerin
forest der Wald
forget vergessen
fork die Gabel
fountain pen der Füller
fourth vierter
France Frankreich
free frei
  (no charge) kostenlos
freezer der Gefrierschrank
French französisch
french fries die Pommes Frites
Frenchman der Franzose

Frenchwoman die Französin
friend der Freund
  (female) die Freundin
friendly freundlich
front: in front of ... vor ...
frost der Frost
fruit die Frucht
fruit juice der Fruchtsaft
fry braten
full voll
  I'm full (up) ich bin satt
full board Vollpension
funny komisch
furniture die Möbel

garage die Garage
garbage der Abfall
garbage bag die Mülltüte
garbage can die Mülltonne
garden der Garten
garlic der Knoblauch
gasoline das Benzin
gas-permeable lenses luftdurchlässige Kontaktlinsen
gas station die Tankstelle
gate das Tor
  (at airport) der Flugsteig
gay *(homosexual)* schwul
gear der Gang
gear shift der Schaltknüppel
gel *(hair)* das Gel
German *(man)* der Deutsche
  (woman) die Deutsche
  (adj.) deutsch
  (language) Deutsch
Germany Deutschland
get *(fetch)* holen
  have you got ...? haben Sie ...?
  to get the train den Zug nehmen
get back: we get back tomorrow wir kommen morgen zurück
  to get something back etwas zurückbekommen

get in hereinkommen
   (arrive) ankommen
get off *(bus, etc.)* aussteigen
get on *(bus, etc.)* einsteigen
get out herauskommen
   (bring out) herausholen
get up *(rise)* aufstehen
gift das Geschenk
gin der Gin
ginger *(spice)* der Ingwer
girl das Mädchen
girlfriend die Freundin
give geben
glad froh
glass das Glas
glasses die Brille
glossy prints die Glanzabzüge
gloves die Handschuhe
glue der Leim
go gehen
   (travel) fahren
   (by plane) fliegen
gold das Gold
good gut
goodbye auf Wiedersehen
government die Regierung
granddaughter die Enkelin
grandfather der Großvater
grandmother die Großmutter
grandparents die Großeltern
grandson der Enkel
grapes die Trauben
grass das Gras
gray grau
great: great! prima! super!
Great Britain Großbritannien
green grün
grocer's das Lebensmittelgeschäft
groundcloth die Bodenplane
ground floor das Erdgeschoß
guarantee *(noun)* die Garantie
   (verb) garantieren
guard der Wächter

guide der Führer
guidebook der (Reise)führer
guitar die Gitarre
gun *(rifle)* das Gewehr
   (pistol) die Pistole

hair das Haar
haircut der Haarschnitt
hair dryer der Fön
hair salon der Friseur
hairspray das Haarspray
half halb
   half an hour eine halbe Stunde
half board Halbpension
ham der gekochte Schinken
hamburger der Hamburger
hammer der Hammer
hand die Hand
handbrake die Handbremse
handkerchief das Taschentuch
handle *(door)* die Klinke
handsome gutaussehend
hangover der Kater
happy glücklich
harbor der Hafen
hard hart
   (difficult) schwer
hard lenses harte Kontaktlinsen
hat der Hut
have haben
   I have ... ich habe ...
   have you got ...? haben Sie ...?
   I have to go ich muß gehen
hay fever der Heuschnupfen
he er
head der Kopf
headache die Kopfschmerzen
headlights die Scheinwerfer
hear hören
hearing aid das Hörgerät
heart das Herz
hearts *(cards)* Herz
heater das Heizgerät

heating die Heizung
heavy schwer
heel *(shoe)* der Absatz
  (foot) die Ferse
hello guten Tag
  (on phone) hallo
help *(noun)* die Hilfe
  (verb) helfen
hepatitis die Hepatitis
her: it's for her es ist für sie
  give it to her geben Sie es ihr
  her book ihr Buch
  her shoes ihre Schuhe
  it's hers es gehört ihr
hi hallo
high hoch
highway die Autobahn
hill der Berg
him: it's for him es ist für ihn
  give it to him geben Sie es ihm
hire leihen, mieten
his: his book sein Buch
  his shoes seine Schuhe
  it's his es gehört ihm
history die Geschichte
hitchhike trampen
HIV positive HIV positiv
hobby das Hobby
Holland Holland
home: at home zu Hause
homeopathy die Homöopathie
honest ehrlich
honey der Honig
honeymoon die Hochzeitsreise
hood *(car)* die Motorhaube
horn *(car)* die Hupe
  (animal) das Horn
horrible schrecklich
hospital das Krankenhaus
hour die Stunde
house das Haus
how? wie?
hungry: I'm hungry ich habe Hunger

hurry: I'm in a hurry ich bin in Eile
husband der (Ehe)mann
I ich
ice das Eis
ice cream das Eis, die Eiscreme
ice skates die Schlittschuhe
ice-skating: to go ice-skating
  Schlittschuhlaufen gehen
if wenn
ignition die Zündung
immediately sofort
impossible unmöglich
in in
  in English auf Englisch
  in the hotel im Hotel
indigestion die Magenverstimmung
inexpensive billig
infection die Infektion
information die Information
inhaler *(for asthma, etc.)* der Inhalierer
injection die Spritze
injury die Verletzung
ink die Tinte
inn das Gasthaus
inner tube der Schlauch
insect das Insekt
insect repellent das Insektenmittel
insomnia die Schlaflosigkeit
instant coffee der Pulverkaffee
insurance die Versicherung
interesting interessant
Internet das Internet
interpret dolmetschen
interpreter der Dolmetscher
  (female) die Dolmetscherin
invitation die Einladung
Ireland Irland
Irish irisch
Irishman der Ire
Irishwoman die Irin
iron *(material)* das Eisen
  (for clothes) das Bügeleisen
  (verb) bügeln

is: he/she/it is … er/sie/es ist …
island die Insel
it es
Italian (man) der Italiener
  (woman) die Italienerin
  (adj.) italienisch
Italy Italien
itch (noun) das Jucken

jacket die Jacke
jam die Marmelade
jazz der Jazz
jeans die Jeans
jellyfish die Qualle
jeweler's das Juweliergeschäft
jewelry der Schmuck
job die Arbeit
jog (verb) joggen
  to go for a jog joggen gehen
joke der Witz
just (only) nur
  it's just arrived es ist gerade
  angekommen

kettle der Wasserkessel
key der Schlüssel
kidney die Niere
kilo das Kilo
kilometer der Kilometer
kitchen die Küche
knee das Knie
knife das Messer
knit stricken
knitwear die Strickwaren
know wissen
  (be acquainted with) kennen
  I don't know ich weiß nicht

label das Etikett
lace die Spitze
laces (shoe) die Schnürsenkel
lady die Dame
lake der See
Lake Constance der Bodensee

lamb (animal) das Lamm
  (meat) das Lammfleisch
lamp die Lampe
lampshade der Lampenschirm
land (noun) das Land
  (verb) landen
language die Sprache
large groß
last (final) letzter
  last week letzte Woche
  at last! endlich!
last name der Nachname
late spät
  the bus is late der Bus hat Verspätung
later später
laugh lachen
Laundromat der Waschsalon
laundry (place) die Wäscherei
  (dirty clothes) die Wäsche
laundry detergent das Waschpulver
laxative das Abführmittel
lazy faul
leadfree bleifrei
leaf das Blatt
leaflet die Broschüre
learn lernen
leather das Leder
left (not right) links
  there's nothing left
  es ist nichts mehr übrig
leg das Bein
lemon die Zitrone
lemonade die Limonade
length die Länge
lens die Linse
less weniger
lesson die Stunde
letter (post) der Brief
  (alphabet) der Buchstabe
letter carrier der Briefträger
lettuce der Kopfsalat
library die Bücherei
license die Genehmigung

license plate das Nummernschild
life das Leben
light *(noun)* das Licht
   (adj.: not heavy) leicht
   (not dark) hell
light bulb die (Glüh)birne
lighter das Feuerzeug
lighter fuel das Feuerzeugbenzin
light meter der Belichtungsmesser
like: I like you ich mag Sie
   I like swimming ich schwimme gern
   it's like … es ist wie …
   like this so
lime *(fruit)* die Limone
line *(noun)* die Schlange
   (verb) anstehen
lip balm der Lippen-Fettstift
lipstick der Lippenstift
liqueur der Likör
list die Liste
liter der Liter
litter der Abfall
little *(small)* klein
   it's a little big es ist ein bißchen
   zu groß
   just a little nur ein bißchen
liver die Leber
lobster der Hummer
lollipop der Lutscher
long lang
lost property das Fundbüro
lot: a lot viel
loud laut
   (color) grell
lounge das Wohnzimmer
   (in hotel) die Lounge
lounge chair der Liegestuhl
love *(noun)* die Liebe
   (verb) lieben
lover *(man)* der Liebhaber
   (woman) die Geliebte
low niedrig
   (voice) tief

luck das Glück
   good luck! viel Glück!
luggage das Gepäck
luggage rack die Gepäckablage
luggage room das Gepäck-schließfach
lunch das Mittagessen
Luxembourg Luxemburg

mad verrückt
magazine die Zeitschrift
mail *(noun)* die Post
   (verb) aufgeben
mailbox der Briefkasten
make machen
make-up das Make-up
man der Mann
manager der Geschäftsführer
many: not many nicht viele
map *(of country)* die Landkarte
   (of town) der Stadtplan
marble der Marmor
margarine die Margarine
market der Markt
marmalade die Orangenmarmelade
married verheiratet
mascara die Wimperntusche
mass *(church)* die Messe
match *(light)* das Streichholz
   (sport) das Spiel
material *(cloth)* der Stoff
matter: it doesn't matter das macht
   nichts
mattress die Matratze
maybe vielleicht
me: it's for me es ist für mich
   give it to me geben Sie es mir
meal das Essen
mean: what does this mean?
   was bedeutet das?
meat das Fleisch
mechanic der Mechaniker
medicine die Medizin
meeting das Treffen

melon die Melone
men *(bathroom)* die Herrentoilette
menu die Speisekarte
message die Nachricht
middle: in the middle in der Mitte
midnight Mitternacht
milk die Milch
mine: it's mine es gehört mir
mineral water das Mineralwasser
minute die Minute
mirror der Spiegel
Miss Fräulein
mistake der Fehler
mobile phone das Mobiltelefon
modem das Modem
mom die Mutter
money das Geld
month der Monat
monument das Denkmal
moon der Mond
moped das Moped
more mehr
morning der Morgen
  in the morning am Morgen
mother die Mutter
motorboat das Motorboot
motorcycle das Motorrad
mountain der Berg
mountain bike das Mountain-Bike
mouse die Maus
mousse *(for hair)* der Schaumfestiger
mouth der Mund
move *(verb)* bewegen
  (house) umziehen
  don't move! stillhalten!
movie der Film
movie theater das Kino
Mr. Herr
Mrs. Frau
Ms. Frau
much viel
Munich München
museum das Museum

mushroom der Pilz
music die Musik
musical instrument das Musikinstrument
musician der Musiker
mussels die Muscheln
must: I must … ich muß …
mustache der Schnurrbart
mustard der Senf
my: my book mein Buch
  my keys meine Schlüssel

nail *(metal, finger)* der Nagel
nail clippers der Nagelzwicker
nailfile die Nagelfeile
nail polish der Nagellack
name der Name
  what's your name? wie heißen Sie?
napkin die Serviette
narrow eng
near nah
  near the door nahe der Tür
  near New York in der Nähe von
  New York
necessary notwendig
neck der Hals
necklace die Halskette
need *(verb)* brauchen
  I need … ich brauche …
  there's no need das ist nicht nötig
needle die Nadel
negative *(photo)* das Negativ
neither: neither of them keiner von
  ihnen
  neither … nor …
  weder … noch …
nephew der Neffe
Netherlands die Niederlande
never nie
new neu
news die Nachrichten
newspaper die Zeitung
newsstand der Zeitungsladen
New Zealand Neuseeland

New Zealander *(man)* der Neuseeländer
  (woman) die Neuseeländerin
next nächster
  next week nächste Woche
nice *(attractive)* hübsch
  (pleasant) angenehm
  (to eat) lecker
niece die Nichte
night die Nacht
nightclub der Nachtklub
nightgown das Nachthemd
night porter der Nachtportier
no *(response)* nein
  I have no money
  ich habe kein Geld
noisy laut
noon der Mittag
north der Norden
Northern Ireland Nordirland
North Sea die Nordsee
nose die Nase
not nicht
notebook das Notizbuch
nothing nichts
novel der Roman
now jetzt
nowhere nirgendwo
nudist der Nudist
number die Zahl
  (telephone) die Nummer
nut *(fruit)* die Nuß
  (for bolt) die Mutter

occasionally gelegentlich
occupied besetzt
of von
  the name of the hotel
  der Name des Hotels
office das Büro
often oft
oil das Öl
ointment die Salbe
OK okay

old alt
  how old are you? wie alt sind Sie?
olive die Olive
omelette das Omelette
on ... auf ...
one *(number)* eins
  one beer/sausage ein Bier/eine Wurst
onion die Zwiebel
only nur
open *(verb)* öffnen
  (adj.) offen
operation die Operation
operator die Vermittlung
opposite: opposite the hotel gegenüber
  dem Hotel
optician der Augenarzt
or oder
orange *(color)* orange
  (fruit) die Orange
orange juice der Orangensaft
orchestra das Orchester
ordinary gewöhnlich
other: the other ... der/die/das andere ...
our unser
  it's ours es gehört uns
out aus
  he's out er ist nicht da
outside außerhalb
oven der Backofen
over *(more than)* über
  (finished) vorbei
  (across) über
  over there dort drüben
oyster die Auster

pacifier der Schnuller
package *(parcel)* das Paket
padlock das Vorhängeschloß
page die Seite
pain der Schmerz
paint *(noun)* die Farbe
pair das Paar
pajamas der Schlafanzug

palace der Palast
pale blaß
pancake der Pfannkuchen
pants die Hose
pantyhose die Strumpfhose
paper das Papier
  (newspaper) die Zeitung
paraffin das Paraffin
parcel das Paket
pardon? bitte?
parents die Eltern
park *(noun)* der Park
  (verb) parken
parsley die Petersilie
part *(hair)* der Scheitel
party *(celebration)* die Party
  (group) die Gruppe
  (political) die Partei
pass *(in car)* überholen
passenger der Passagier
passport der Paß
pasta die Nudeln
pastry shop die Konditorei
path der Weg
pavement der Bürgersteig
pay bezahlen
peach der Pfirsich
peanuts die Erdnüsse
pear die Birne
pearl die Perle
peas die Erbsen
pedestrian der Fußgänger
pen der Stift
pencil der Bleistift
pencil sharpener der Bleistiftspitzer
pen pal der Brieffreund
  (female) die Brieffreundin
people die Leute
pepper der Pfeffer
  (red/green) der Paprika
peppermints die Pfefferminzbonbons
per: per night pro Nacht
perfect perfekt

perfume das Parfüm
perhaps vielleicht
perm die Dauerwelle
pharmacy die Apotheke
phone book das Telefonbuch
phonecard die Telefonkarte
photocopier der Fotokopierer
photograph *(noun)* das Foto
  (verb) fotografieren
photographer der Fotograf
phrase book der Sprachführer
piano das Klavier
pickpocket der Taschendieb
picnic das Picknick
piece das Stück
pillow das Kopfkissen
pilot der Pilot
pin die Stecknadel
  (clothes) die Wäscheklammer
pineapple die Ananas
pink rosa
pipe *(for smoking)* die Pfeife
  (for water) das Rohr
piston der Kolben
pizza die Pizza
place der Platz
  (town, etc.) der Ort
  at your place bei Ihnen
plant die Pflanze
plastic das Plastik
plastic bag die Plastiktüte
plastic wrap die Folie
plate der Teller
platform der Bahnsteig
play *(theater)* das Stück
  (verb) spielen
please bitte
plug *(electrical)* der Stecker
  (sink) der Stöpsel
pocket die Tasche
pocketbook die Handtasche
pocketknife das Taschenmesser
poison das Gift

Poland Polen
Pole *(man)* der Pole
  (woman) die Polin
Polish polnisch
police die Polizei
police officer der Polizist
police station das Polizeirevier
politics die Politik
poor arm
  (bad quality) schlecht
pop music die Popmusik
pork das Schweinefleisch
port *(harbor)* der Hafen
  (drink) der Portwein
porter *(hotel)* der Portier
possible möglich
postcard die Postkarte
poster das Poster
post office das Postamt
potato die Kartoffel
potato chips die Chips
poultry das Geflügel
pound *(weight)* das Pfund
powder das Pulver
  (cosmetics) das Puder
prefer: I prefer …
  ich mag lieber …
prescription das Rezept
pretty *(beautiful)* schön
  (quite) ziemlich
  pretty good
  recht gut
priest der Geistliche
private privat
problem das Problem
public öffentlich
pull ziehen
puncture die Reifenpanne
purple lila
purse das Portemonnaie
push drücken
put legen, stellen, setzen

quality die Qualität
quarter das Viertel
question die Frage
quick schnell
quiet ruhig
quite *(fairly)* ziemlich
  (fully) ganz

radiator der Heizkörper
  (car) der Kühler
radio das Radio
radish der Rettich
  (small red) das Radieschen
railroad die Bahn
rain der Regen
rain boots die Gummistiefel
raincoat der Regenmantel
raisins die Rosinen
rare *(uncommon)* selten
  (steak) englisch
raspberries die Himbeeren
rat die Ratte
razor blades die Rasierklingen
read lesen
reading lamp die Leselampe
ready fertig
receipt die Quittung
receptionist die Empfangsperson
record *(music)* die Schallplatte
  (sports, etc.) der Rekord
record player der Plattenspieler
record store das Schallplattengeschäft
red rot
refreshments die Erfrischungen
refrigerator der Kühlschrank
relative der Verwandte
relax sich entspannen
religion die Religion
remember sich erinnern
  I don't remember ich erinnere mich
  nicht
rent *(verb)* mieten
reservation die Reservierung

rest *(noun: remainder)* der Rest
  (verb: relax) sich ausruhen
restaurant das Restaurant
return *(come back)* zurückkommen
  (give back) zurückgeben
rice der Reis
rich reich
right *(correct)* richtig
  (direction) rechts
ring *(wedding, etc.)* der Ring
ripe reif
river der Fluß
road die Straße
rock *(stone)* der Stein
  (music) der Rock
roll *(bread)* das Brötchen
roof das Dach
room das Zimmer
  (space) der Raum
rope das Seil
rose die Rose
round *(circular)* rund
  it's my round das ist meine Runde
round-trip ticket die Rückfahrkarte
rowboat das Ruderboot
rubber *(material)* das Gummi
rubber band das Gummiband
ruby *(stone)* der Rubin
rug *(mat)* der Läufer
  (blanket) die Wolldecke
ruins die Ruinen
ruler *(for drawing)* das Lineal
rum der Rum
run *(verb)* laufen
runway die Start-und Landebahn

sad traurig
safe sicher
safety pin die Sicherheitsnadel
sailboat das Segelboot
salad der Salat
salami die Salami
sale *(at reduced prices)* der Schlußverkauf

salmon der Lachs
salt das Salz
same: the same dress das gleiche Kleid
  same again, please nochmal dasselbe,
  bitte
sand der Sand
sandals die Sandalen
sandwich das Butterbrot
sanitary napkins die Damenbinden
sauce die Soße
saucepan der Kochtopf
sauna die Sauna
sausage die Wurst
say sagen
  what did you say? was haben Sie
  gesagt?
  how do you say …? wie sagt
  man …?
Scandinavia Skandinavien
scarf der Schal
  (head) das Kopftuch
school die Schule
scissors die Schere
Scotland Schottland
Scotsman der Schotte
Scotswoman die Schottin
Scottish schottisch
screw die Schraube
screwdriver der Schraubenzieher
sea das Meer
seafood die Meeresfrüchte
seat der Sitz
seat belt der Sicherheitsgurt
second *(time)* die Sekunde
  (in series) zweiter
see sehen
  I can't see ich kann nichts sehen
  I see ich verstehe
sell verkaufen
separate getrennt
separately getrennt
separated: we are separated wir leben
  getrennt

serious ernst
several mehrere
sew nähen
shampoo das Shampoo
shave: to have a shave sich rasieren
shaving cream die Rasiercreme
shawl das Umhängetuch
she sie
sheet das (Bett)laken
shell die Muschel
shellfish (as food) die Meeresfrüchte
sherry der Sherry
ship das Schiff
shirt das Hemd
shoelaces die Schnürsenkel
shoe polish die Schuhcreme
shoes die Schuhe
shopping das Einkaufen
  (items bought) die Einkäufe
  to go shopping
  einkaufen gehen
short kurz
shorts die Shorts
shoulder die Schulter
shower (bath) die Dusche
  (rain) der Schauer
shower gel das Duschgel
shrimp die Garnelen
shutter (camera) der Verschluß
  (window) der Fensterladen
sick (ill) krank
  I feel sick mir ist übel
  to be sick (vomit) sich übergeben
side die Seite
  (edge) die Kante
sidelights das Standlicht
sights: the sights of ... die
  Sehenswürdigkeiten von ...
silk die Seide
silver (color) silber
  (metal) das Silber
simple einfach
sing singen

single (one) einziger
  (unmarried) ledig, single
single room das Einzelzimmer
sister die Schwester
ski (verb) Ski fahren
ski binding die Skibindung
ski boots die Skistiefel
skid (verb) schleudern
skiing: to go skiing Skifahren gehen
ski lift der Skilift
skin cleanser der Hautreiniger
ski poles die Skistöke
ski resort der Skiurlaubsort
skillet die (Brat)pfanne
skirt der Rock
skis die Skier
sky der Himmel
sled der Schlitten
sleep (noun) der Schlaf
  (verb) schlafen
sleeping bag der Schlafsack
sleeping pill die Schlaftablette
slippers die Pantoffeln
slow langsam
small klein
smell (noun) der Geruch
  (verb) riechen
smile (noun) das Lächeln
  (verb) lächeln
smoke (noun) der Rauch
  (verb) rauchen
snack der Imbiß
sneakers die Turnschuhe
snow der Schnee
so so
  not so much nicht so viel
soaking solution (for contact lenses) die
  Aufbewahrungslösung
soap die Seife
soccer der Fußball
socks die Socken
soda water das Sodawasser
soft lenses weiche Kontaktlinsen

somebody jemand

somehow irgendwie

something etwas

sometimes manchmal

somewhere irgendwo

son der Sohn

song das Lied

sorry! *(apology)* Verzeihung!

  I'm sorry es tut mir leid

  sorry? *(pardon)* bitte?

soup die Suppe

south der Süden

South Africa Südafrika

souvenir das Souvenir

spa der Kurort

spade *(shovel)* der Spaten

spades *(cards)* Pik

spare parts die Ersatzteile

spark plug die Zündkerze

speak sprechen

  do you speak English? sprechen Sie
  Englisch?

  I don't speak German ich spreche
  kein Deutsch

speed die Geschwindigkeit

spider die Spinne

spinach der Spinat

spoon der Löffel

sports center das Sportzentrum

spring *(mechanical)* die Feder

  (season) der Frühling

square *(shape)* das Quadrat

  (in town) der Platz

stadium das Stadion

staircase die Treppe

stairs die Treppe

stamp die Briefmarke

stapler der Hefter

star der Stern

  (movie) der Star

start der Start, der Anfang

  (verb) anfangen

station der Bahnhof

  (subway) die Station

statue die Statue

steak das Steak

steal stehlen

  it's been stolen es
  ist gestohlen worden

steamer *(boat)* der Dampfer

  (cooking) der Dampfkochtopf

steering wheel das Lenkrad

sting *(noun)* der Stich

  (verb) stechen

stockings die Strümpfe

stomach der Magen

stomachache die Magenschmerzen

stop *(bus stop)* die Haltestelle

  (verb) anhalten

  stop! halt!

store das Geschäft

storm der Sturm

stove der Herd

strawberries die Erdbeeren

stream *(small river)* der Bach

street die Straße

string *(cord)* der Faden

  (guitar, etc.) die Saite

stroller der Sportwagen

strong *(person, drink)* stark

  (material) stabil

  (taste) streng

student der Student

  (female) die Studentin

stupid dumm

suburbs der Stadtrand

subway die U-Bahn

sugar der Zucker

suit *(noun)* der Anzug

  it suits you es steht Ihnen

suitcase der Koffer

sun die Sonne

sunbathe sonnenbaden

sunburn der Sonnenbrand

sunglasses die Sonnenbrille

sunny: it's sunny es ist sonnig

sunshade der Sonnenschirm
suntan: to get a suntan braun werden
suntan lotion das Sonnenöl
suntanned braungebrannt
supermarket der Supermarkt
supper das Abendessen
supplement der Zuschlag
sure sicher
suspenders die Hosenträger
sweat *(noun)* der Schweiß
   (verb) schwitzen
sweater der Pullover
sweatshirt das Sweatshirt
sweet *(not sour)* süß
swim *(verb)* schwimmen
swimming pool das Schwimmbad
swimsuit das Badekostüm
Swiss *(man)* der Schweizer
   (woman) die Schweizerin
   (adj.) schweizerisch
switch der Schalter
Switzerland die Schweiz
synagogue die Synagoge

table der Tisch
tablet die Tablette
taillights die Rücklichter
take nehmen
takeoff der Abflug
take out der Schnellimbiß
talcum powder das Körperpuder
talk *(noun)* das Gespräch
   (verb) reden
tall groß
tampons die Tampons
tangerine die Mandarine
tap der Hahn
tapestry der Wandteppich
tea der Tee
teacher der Lehrer
   (female) die Lehrerin
telephone *(noun)* das Telefon
   (verb) telefonieren

telephone booth die Telefonzelle
television das Fernsehen
   to watch television fernsehen
temperature die Temperatur
   (fever) das Fieber
tent das Zelt
tent pole die Zeltstange
tent stake der Hering
than: bigger than größer als
thank *(verb)* danken
   thanks danke
   thank you danke schön
that: that man dieser Mann
   that woman diese Frau
   what's that? was ist das?
   I think that … ich denke, daß …
the der, die, das
   (pl.) die
their: their room ihr Zimmer
   their books ihre Bücher
   it's theirs es gehört ihnen
them: it's for them es ist für sie
   give it to them geben Sie es ihnen
then dann
there da
   there is/are … es gibt …
   is/are there …? gibt es …?
these diese
they sie
thick dick
thin dünn
think denken
   I think so ich glaube ja
   I'll think about it ich überlege es mir
third dritter
thirsty durstig
   I'm thirsty ich habe Durst
this: this man dieser Mann
   this woman diese Frau
   what's this? was ist das?
   this is Mr. … das ist Herr …
those diese da
   those things die Dinge dort

141

throat die Kehle
through durch
thumbtack die Heftwecke
thunderstorm das Gewitter
ticket die Karte
tide: high tide die Flut
  low tide die Ebbe
tie *(noun)* die Krawatte
  (verb) festmachen
tight eng
time die Zeit
  what's the time? wie spät ist es?
timetable *(train, bus)* der Fahrplan
tip *(money)* das Trinkgeld
  (end) die Spitze
tire *(on car)* der Reifen
tired müde
tissues die Papiertaschentücher
to: to America nach Amerika
  to the station zum Bahnhof
  to the doctor zum Arzt
toast der Toast
tobacco der Tabak
toboggan der Schlitten
today heute
together zusammen
toilet die Toilette
toilet paper das Toilettenpapier
tomato die Tomate
tomato juice der Tomatensaft
tomorrow morgen
tongue die Zunge
tonic das Tonic
tonight heute abend
too *(also)* auch
  (excessively) zu
tooth der Zahn
toothache die Zahnschmerzen
toothbrush die Zahnbürste
toothpaste die Zahnpasta
tour die Rundreise
tour guide der Reiseleiter
  (female) die Reiseleiterin

tourist der Tourist
  (female) die Touristin
tourist office
  das Fremdenverkehrsbüro
towel das Handtuch
tower der Turm
town die Stadt
town hall das Rathaus
toy das Spielzeug
track suit der Trainingsanzug
tractor der Traktor
tradition die Tradition
traffic der Verkehr
traffic jam der Stau
traffic lights die Ampel
trailer der Anhänger
train der Zug
translate übersetzen
translator der Übersetzer
  (female) die Übersetzerin
travel agency das Reisebüro
traveler's check der Reisescheck
tray das Tablett
tree der Baum
trip die Reise
truck der Lastwagen
true wahr
try versuchen
tunnel der Tunnel
Turk *(man)* der Türke
  (woman) die Türkin
Turkey die Türkei
Turkish türkisch
turn signal der Blinker
tweezers die Pinzette
typewriter die Schreibmaschine

umbrella der (Regen)schirm
uncle der Onkel
under ... unter ...
underpants die Unterhose
undershirt das (Unter)hemd
underskirt der Unterrock

understand verstehen
 I don't understand
 ich verstehe nicht
underwear die Unterwäsche
university die Universität
unleaded bleifrei
until bis
unusual ungewöhnlich
up oben
 (upward) nach oben
 up there da oben
urgent dringend
us: it's for us es ist für uns
 give it to us geben Sie es uns
use *(noun)* der Gebrauch
 (verb) gebrauchen
 it's no use es hat keinen Zweck
useful hilfreich
usual gewöhnlich
usually gewöhnlich

vacancy *(room)* ein freies Zimmer
vacation der Urlaub
vacuum cleaner der Staubsauger
valley das Tal
valve das Ventil
vanilla die Vanille
vase die Vase
VCR der Videorecorder
veal das Kalbfleisch
vegetable das Gemüse
vegetarian der Vegetarier
 (female) die Vegetarierin
 (adj.) vegetarisch
vehicle das Fahrzeug
very sehr
video *(tape, film)* das Video
Vienna Wien
view der Blick
viewfinder der Sucher
villa die Villa
village das Dorf
vinegar der Essig

violin die Violine
visit *(noun)* der Besuch
 (verb) besuchen
visitor der Besucher
 (female) die Besucherin
vitamin pill die Vitamintablette
vodka der Wodka
voice die Stimme

wait warten
 wait! warten Sie!
waiter der Ober
 waiter! Herr Ober!
waiting room das Wartezimmer
 (station) der Wartesaal
waitress die Kellnerin
 waitress! Fräulein!
Wales Wales
walk *(noun: stroll)* der Spaziergang
 (verb) gehen
 to go for a walk spazieren gehen
wall *(inside)* die Wand
 (outside) die Mauer
wallet die Brieftasche
war der Krieg
wardrobe der Kleiderschrank
warm warm
was: I was ich war
 he/she/it was er/sie/es warr
wasp die Wespe
watch *(noun)* die (Armband)uhr
 (verb) ansehen
water das Wasser
waterfall der Wasserfall
water heater das Heißwassergerät
wave *(noun)* die Welle
 (verb: with hand) winken
wavy *(hair)* wellig
we wir
weather das Wetter
website die Webseite
wedding die Hochzeit
week die Woche

143

welcome willkommen
  you're welcome keine Ursache
Welsh walisisch
Welshman der Waliser
Welshwoman die Waliserin
were: we/they were wir/sie waren
  you were Sie waren
  (sing., familiar) du warst
west der Westen
wet naß
what? was?
wheel das Rad
wheelchair der Rollstuhl
when? wann?
where? wo?
whether ob
which? welcher?
whiskey der Whisky
white weiß
who? wer?
why? warum?
wide breit
wife die (Ehe)frau
wind der Wind
window das Fenster
wine der Wein
wing der Flügel
with mit
without ohne
woman die Frau
women *(bathroom)* die Damentoilette
wood *(material)* das Holz
wool die Wolle

word das Wort
work *(noun)* die Arbeit
  (verb) arbeiten
  (machine, etc.) funktionieren
worse schlechter
worst schlechtester
wrapping paper das Packpapier
  (for presents) das Geschenkpapier
wrench der Schraubenschlüssel
wrist das Handgelenk
writing paper das Schreibpapier
wrong falsch

year das Jahr
yellow gelb
yes ja
yesterday gestern
yet: is it ready yet? ist es schon fertig?
  not yet noch nicht
yogurt der Joghurt
you Sie
  (sing., familiar) du
  for you für Sie/dich
  with you mit Ihnen/dir
your Ihr
  (sing., familiar) dein
  your shoes Ihre/deine Schuhe
yours: is this yours? gehört das Ihnen?
  (familiar) gehört das dir?
youth hostel die Jugendherberge

zipper der Reißverschluß
zoo der Zoo